INDIAN
An Ideal Labour or Slave

INDIAN

An Ideal Labour or Slave

Krishnan Arunachalam

Foreword by

V.R. Lakshminarayanan, IPS

Former Director-General of Police of Tamilnadu, Director of CBI and presently the Chair person of Bharathiya Vidya Bhavan, Chennai Chapter

PENTAGON PRESS

INDIAN: An Ideal Labour or Slave

First Published in 2009 by

PENTAGON PRESS
206, Peacock Lane, Shahpur Jat, New Delhi-110049
Phones: 011-64706243, 26491568
Telefax: 011-26490600
email: rajan@pentagon-press.com
website: www.pentagon-press.com

Co-Published with

ARIES BOOKS INTERNATIONAL
No. 10 Venkataraman Street, Srinivasa Avenue,
R.A. Puram, Chennai 600 028. India

ISBN 978-81-8274-393-9

Printed at New Elegant Printers, New Delhi.

Dedicated to

My father

Late R.S. Krishnan

Central Intelligence Officer

Ministry of Home affairs

Foreword

"History" wrote Voltaire, " is nothing more than a tableau of crimes and misfortunes". We have here a history of India – social, military, political and economic, form medieval times to the IT explosions pitch forking India into global prominence and world power pretensions. The account is as interesting as Friedman's—"The world is Flat". While the American is ecstatic and wrote with the school boyish joy infecting every reader with his sense of wonderment and dream, Arunachalam pours different cup of Indian tea. One cannot escape a certain sense of cynicism in his prognosis in reporting that globalization and its aftermath can turn both India and China into a paradise or one does not know whether it will be a new kind of glorified serfdom turning back the clock. India has weathered many storms and tsunamis and we not only survive but lead the rest of the world. That needs spiritual strength more than material wealth and the land of Ghandhiji, Buddha and Vivekananda can triumph over the challenges from the West. Annu's warnings are real and cannot be dismissed lightly. This book is worth reading, for it splashes some cold water on our self-satisfied faces and gives us a timely warning of the perils miscalled prosperity. It would have added considerably to the merit of this stupendous work, had the author suggested some remedies to arrest the slow slide in the quality of our emerging university products who are in the vanguard of our global success but slowly making headway backwards. The old euphoria is waning and greater energy need to be pumped in.

That apart the prose is delectable and the facts dredged out are indicative of the pains taken by the author. A readable work of great merit.

V.R. Lakshminarayanan, IPS

Prologue

The migration of people from one place to another whether within or between the countries have been a point of attraction, debate and discussion for centuries.

Migration vertical and horizontal has been a great help in developing and building the nations. There has been for variety of reasons for migration ranging from economic, cultural and social factors.

India has been seen a very attractive point in others words, a hub for supplying labour in different parts of the world, the reason being hard working talented and cheap labour. There is no doubt that Indians have helped a lot in developing nations and societies but on the other hand it has its side effects too. There have been several studies on reasons for migration of workers and or pattern of migration within the country and between the countries. However, no systematic study is available about the history of migrant Indians to different parts of the world. This book is an honest attempt to explore India's details of migration and its typology to different countries starting from the era of Mohammed Bin Qasim in 9th century to the BPOs/KPOs of 21st century.

The book is divided in 26 chapters whilst the 1 and 2 chapter highlights the slavery period of India, the 3 and 4 chapters discuss about the various slaves and alternative to slaves that is in "indentured labour" in the post 1833 scenario.

These chapters present a very descriptive picture of slavery across the globe. However, the chapters 5 to 12 present the heart felt depiction of Coolies, across the world in very systematic way.

These chapters highlight Coolies in different parts of the world like Caribbean, Mauritius, East Africa, South Africa South-east Asia, Australia and New Zealand and western world like America (USA) and Canada. This is quiet evident from the discussion that there is common thread across the globe that connects the slaves of India with the rest of the world.

The book in its subsequent discussion presents other dimensions of forced labour like Lashkar, it further elaborates migration of Ayahs and Nurses as well. The Chapter 16, provides the detailed information about "indentured soldiers" in world-war I and II, which were subsequently legalized in India and Gulf as well.

The author with his experience of about 27 countries across the globe presents a very meaningful depiction of forced labour and advocates that India has been always trapped in slavery whether it is of the ancient period or modern period. This has been due to lack of appropriate understanding as well as planning of resources.

The author carefully emphasizes on the fact that BPOs/ KPOs are similar to indentured labour (CYBER COOLIE) within India which will be a replica of East India Company. The author discusses with the suitable examples about all these in chapter 22 to 24. The author further warned about the side effects of brain-drain and alarming attrition rate in BPO and KPO sector. Chapter 25 with "Dynamite under the dream" exposes about these developments in India.

Chapter 26, very interestingly explains about technology, which is dominated by Multinational Companies sitting in USA and UK, are likely to dominate Indian scenario in future.

The author fears, very rightly, about possibilities of India being puppet of USA and UK in near future.

The conclusion part of the book, indicates that there is a boom in the economy due to MNCs but the author doubts whether we are economically independent? The country like India where 55% of GDP is from the service sector can not be seen as safe and secure.

"Finally, the author deserves congratulations for writing such master piece as theme, which is of a great interest to world in general and to the India in particular."

D.K. Srivastava

Introduction

Is Dasan, The Destiny of Desis?

Migration is a very euphemistic word to describe the movement of people from one place to another. The process of migration makes all the difference. Power politics, economic prosperity and social/religious oppression are the general reasons for migration from one country or continent to another. Europeans moved out of their continent to the Americas in search of wealth and later became conquerors, Jews moved out of Germany to escape persecution by the Nazis, Hindus moved from North India to south of India due to the religious fanaticism of the invading Muslim kings from Central Asia. Traders moved to different places for marketing their goods. Past history reveals that it was military might that paved the way for migration.

It may not be appropriate to describe the presence of African Americans in the Americas as migration from the African continent. Their population in USA, Caribbean, and Latin America is more than 10% of the total. They did not come to the other side of the Atlantic Ocean on their own; they were brought in by force that too in chains. They were imported as slaves and traded like commodities. Although they had the option to go back to Africa they stayed where they were as they almost lost the trace of their roots. Many would have even preferred the new country as their ultimate place for economic/social/religious reasons.

There was no clear evidence of Indian migration to other countries although we had very good trade relationships with the Romans, Arabs and Chinese. It may be largely due to the religious belief that crossing the ocean (Kala Pani) was considered a sin. Indians are no better than the blacks of Africa. Indians are now spread out from Trinidad (West Indies) to Wellington in New Zealand. This so called migration happened under the authority of the British who ruled India for 200 years. Wherever the flag of Union Jack (British flag) flew you will find Indians there. The serfdom image imposed on the Indians for the last 7 centuries is still not removed even after 60 years of independence. Current globalization drives and its acceptance by India reconfirms the status of Indians as the most obedient and efficient servants.

Past history, reveals that we had been very submissive to foreigners and offered ourselves to be their servants. I traced different stages of our history beginning with the medieval age (500 years ago) and realized that at every stage we were subdued and forced to work for foreigners either in our own country or elsewhere. It is very unfortunate that there is no record of Indian migration to many of the Far Eastern countries where the Indian culture, language (Sanskrit) and religions (Hindu and Buddhist) were predominant for over 5 centuries. Diaspora studies mention the movements of Indians as migration; history shows that the migration started only after the arrival of Europeans. Indians migrated to various parts of the world only as slaves or labourers.

This book gives information about the Indian labour's service in foreign countries and to the foreigners inside India. This is not an exclusive study of Diaspora but the traditional and modern slavery imposed on Indians which they have accepted. The Indian Diaspora is viewed from a different angle.

The nation's local submission to foreign invaders and their exploitation of our wealth and resources (except labour) does not come under the purview of this book.

This book traces the events and circumstances under which Indians were enslaved for 700 years under the brutal occupation of invaders from Middle East starting from the invasion of Mohamed Bin Qasim in 900 AD; followed by the ruthless and greedy European merchants during 1600 to 1800 AD. They became legalized slaves (Indentured workers) under the British rule for 150 years and served as garden coolies, lascars and soldiers. Indian women were also enslaved as ayahs and nurses. As detailed information is available from records and documents vivid description is made about the Indentureship of Indians.

In 20th century Indians continued to be slaves even after becoming independent. Indentureship of Indians was legalised and globalised by free Indian governments since 1970 AD. In the late 20th century cyber revolution brought back the same coolie scenario of 19th century. We have completed 1000 years as able servants (Dasan) to foreigners. A trial analysis is made to find out whether it is our destiny.

Contents

CHAPTER 1

Indian Slavery Ancient India

Indian culture adores loyalty to service. This may be due to fear and insecurity. Yajamana viswasam (Servitude) was hailed as a great virtue in our culture. Probably this led to the slavish attitude of the Indians who for the last eight centuries had been living in their own country serving for the foreigners. Their eagerness to serve foreigners has its own reasons. The individualistic feeling which is inherent in the minds of every Indian and his/her disregard for organization or community growth may be the main reasons for their bent of mind. A.S.P. Iyer in his book "Rambles in Literature, Art, Law and Philosophy" rightly pointed out the difference between the Western society and Indian society. He describes that in the west the society is in the centre and the family in the circumference whereas in the Indian society the family in the centre and the society in the circumference. Is it the Hindu religion that laid the foundation for these feelings? The answer is no. Even the converted Christians and Muslims are also part of this process. It may be the inherent nature of the people born in India or Indians born elsewhere but of Indian origin. Probably it is the Indian gene that generates this attitude and approach. Is it due to Fear of god or any supernatural forces?

Is it due to the inherent attitude of living happily with what is available? Accept a life as it comes without the aggressiveness or the eagerness to further enhance the lifestyle? Strong resistance and reluctance to change in the social, economic and political life is a common feature in the Indian society. Is it due to lack of innovation or laziness? There is a saying that "if Rama rules, it is Ramaya Namaha;if Ravana rules it is Ravanaya Namaha". Enjoy the life with least botheration about achievement or better living except the accumulation of gold and gold jewelry. It is still a puzzle that the situation on the basic principles of serving others remains strong despite the scientific and technological developments. Independence from the harsh Mogul rule or the exploitative British rule had not improved the condition. Is it a curse or gift of God? There could also be another reason that the society is basically a village society and urban life was limited to few pockets here and there. Centralized administration was totally absent right from the days of Mauryan rule until the advent of the British. The unity was mostly based on religious binding, which in turn developed into a strong cultural unification.

Slavery was not practiced in ancient India. The dictionary meaning of slavery is "a person is dominated by a specific thing or person". "A servant completely divested of freedom and personal rights." The Sanskrit translation for slave is "Dasan". The inner meaning of Dasan in olden days denoted to devotion to God. The word "Das" which comes from Dasan and generally attached to a God/Goddess or a noble act. Ancient India had developed caste system based on the responsibilities of individuals to the stability and standing of a village community. Indian scholars and historians are of the opinion that slavery was a recognized institution of Indian society from the oldest Vedic times. The smrithis distinguish between different classes of slaves and also the rules regarding their status. According to Narada and Manu, slaves could be acquired by birth in the master's house, purchase, gift, inheritance, maintenance during famine, pledge, release from a heavy debt, capture in war, gain in wager, voluntary surrender of freedom, apostasy from asceticism, connection with a female slave and through other process. Slavery was also one among various judicial punishments for crime. The slaves according to Narada are to perform impure works. A slave is not entitled to property according to Manu. Even legal acts of slaves are void unless they were done with the permission of the master according to Manu. Narada indicated that a debt incurred by the slave on behalf of the master is binding upon him. Narada and Yagyavalkia laid down the rules for emancipation of slaves. A slave who saved the master's life is immediately released and takes up the status of master's son. The master could release the slaves any time at his will.

The Sastras and a few epics, speak openly about slavery, but there is no historical evidence of the practice of slavery in India. According to Megasthenes "all the Indians are free and not one of them is a slave" He simplified that "Indians do not even use the aliens as slaves and much less a countryman of their own." There are so many references to the system of slavery in the Smirithis and literature that is difficult to accept Megasthenese's statement. Slaves in India were generally household servants and not badly treated and their numbers seem insignificant". Such mild treatment, which offered a striking, contrast to the system of slavery with which Magasthenese was familiar probably led him to believe that there were no slaves in India.

Many historians have highlighted the remarks of Megasthenese while writing about Indian history, the western historians however tried to establish a connection between the lower cast of the society with that of slaves. The lower caste although treated inhumanly, deprived of many privileges and condemned as untouchables, was not as sub human as the slavery practiced by the Romans and the Turkish. Although the society was divided by the caste system slavery was not practiced in India as badly as in the West or Muslim countries. Neither the epics nor any historical studies ever highlighted the existence of slavery. In most literature the word slave was used only to denote their devotion to god or any human practices like drinking or smoking or womanizing. It was more of habits and devotion rather than human slavery.

Slavery was first introduced in India by the invaders of the medieval period. Slavery was unknown even during Alexander's invasion and his conquest of northwestern parts of India. Slavery was disapproved by all the religions originated from India like Hinduism, Jainism and Buddhism. Well-known and traditional traders from Gujarat and Marwar never indulged in this trade although it was prevailing extensively in north India for 6 centuries. Historian Moreland mentioned that in 1643 AD when a Nayak chief was offered 1000 slave by the Dutch East India Company he rejected the offer saying that sale of a human being is not only a scandal but also a sin.

CHAPTER 2

Indian Slavery During the Medieval Period

Pry into the history one could find the awash with horrifying tales of cruelty and humiliation unleashed by the invading Muslim kings in India. However we can not rule exaggeration by the English historical writers who revealed this information in the form of their findings in various research papers. Many of them were biased towards the Indians and their rich culture, which remained un conquerable, even by waves of foreign invasion for the last 9 centuries. It all began with a young and dynamic Iraqi called Muhammad bin Qasim plundering Sindh province and paving the way for the Muslim domination of India in the year 900 AD. It was also the beginning of slave trade in India.

Following is the gist of some interesting information given by K.S. Lal in his book "Muslim Slave System in Medieval India" describing the process and functioning of slavery in India during the reign of the Muslim kings from Persia and Arab countries.

It is believed that Muhammad bin Qasim captured 20,000 Indians as slaves in his military expedition in Sindh. The slaves were sorted out on the basis of looks for the women, physical fitness and craftsmanship for men. Amir Timur who invaded India in 1399 took a large number of slaves who were classified as artisans and clever mechanics. The skilled stonemasons and builders were taken away to Samarkand where he wanted to build a masjid Majid-i-jami that was intended to stand as a great mosque unrivaled by others in any country. Most of the Indian slaves were prisoners of war. They were generally sold to the Amirs and Nobles of the conqueror.

The notorious Mohammed Ghazni carried away a large number of slaves from India and sold them in the open market. The captives of his campaign in Mathura and Kanauj numbering 53,000 were sold for two to ten Dhirams in the open market. Slave traders from different parts gathered in the cities to make their purchase. Mohammad Ghazni brought over 200,000 prisoners as slaves from his plunder of Thaneshwar in India. The number of prisoners was more than his army. The city of Ghazni was filled with Indian slaves (like Dubai, Riyadh and Kuwait in recent years). The price of these slaves followed the economic theory of supply and demand. Some historians bluntly commented that Mohammed of Ghazni made more money by selling the Indian slaves in the open market than by plundering several temples in India.

Indian slave trade further expanded during the regime of the Delhi Sultanate. Slaves were generally used for clearing jungles, laying roads, doing errand service for the army personnel, civil constructions and as camp servants. The Muslim Kings and Nobles hired several slaves for their household chores. Slave girls were used for pleasure and other services. Slaves were also gifted as a mark of courtesy. Sultan Alaudin Khilji the notorious king of Delhi was known to be very keen after military expedition in selling the captives on the spot and in the Delhi market. Alaudin Khilji, known for his brutal price control procedure, fixed the price for slaves as for any other commodity. The price of an ordinary man (Ghulam) was around 100 to 200 Tanakas depending upon his age and physical fitness. A good-looking girl suitable to be a concubine fetched more than others. The price of a young boy or girl (Ghulam Bachgan Naukri) was around 50 to 70 Tanakas. Special prices were fixed for bulk purchases. Alaudin Khiliji controlled the slave market himself, as it was very lucrative. Historian T.P. Hughes mentions that the slaves were treated on par with commodities. The general rules that were applied in the sale and purchase of animals were followed in the human slave market. Buffalos or milk-producing cattle were sometimes priced more than a young girl. A good quality horse or camel would cost more than a Ghulam. Captives who were identified as royal family members or associated with royal family were separated and sent to the court for royal services.

The road running from Delhi to Lahore and Khandahar and finally ending at Kabul had hundreds of caravans every week carrying Indian slaves to the various markets in Afganistan and Iran. Historian Willam Finch writes that hunting of men of the jungle was on the same footing as beasts and handed over to the king. It was also mentioned that men were exchanged for horses and dogs. Bartering human slaves for commodities and animals was not uncommon during the medieval days. There were many centers for slave trade and the most notable among these were Delhi, Badaon in UP and Mandor in Rajastan.

CHAPTER 3

Indian Slavery European Period

During the earlier colonial days the English, French, Dutch and Portuguese were engaged in the slave trade. The English paid an average of 40 to 50 rupees a slave whereas the Dutch paid more. The Dutch were very active, as they needed men for their plantation in Indonesia, particularly, those trained and experienced in the spice fields. They were regularly buying slaves from India. Many imported slaves were 'Bengaldhars (Bengalis), Arakandars (people in the Indo Burmese border) and Malabars (Keralites). Many of the slaves were reported to have died due to change in the weather and living conditions. Foreign slaves from Mangolia and Uzbek were also available in the market and they used to fetch more than the Indians. Bargaining for better price was very common in the slave market. Bulk purchases were settled immediately. Merchants from Turkey, Syria, and Persia regularly visited Delhi with their consignments. Foreign slaves, both men and women, were in great demand in India. Slavery was widespread in the Islamic countries as the religion approved the practice. It was a pride for the Delhi sultans to have foreign slaves. Among the Europeans, the Portuguese were notorious like the Muslim kings. They regularly indulged in slave trade. Della Valle mentioned that Portuguese regularly brought slaves from Abyssinia and Mozambique. According to him the greatest part of people in Goa were slaves. The Portuguese dominated the Arabian Sea for a century and had possession of the Strait of Hormuz, a strategic point in the gulf of Persia. The Portuguese governor once infuriated Shajahan, the Mogul emperor by snatching his boats and capturing some of Mumtaz Mahall's slave girls. Shajahan after becoming the Mogul King ordered the Mogul governor in Bengal to expel the trading Portuguese. Portuguese were beaten in the battle against the Moguls and were expelled from Bengal.

African slaves brought in were known as Sidi or Habshi. Most of them were brought in as slaves to serve the Muslim kings and noble men either for domestic purpose or as security guards. They were hired as personal attendants or personal bodyguards since servants having no local blood or connections would ensure loyalty and safety. They were sunny Muslims from Ethiopia, Kenya and Zanzibar;a few were brought in by Indian merchants who returned after a long tenure in the Middle East or Africa. This is similar to the Ayahs taken by the retiring British officers who returned to England with their trusted Indian Ayahs. The famous Anandharangam Pillai who functioned as the right hand for Joseph Duplix, the French Governor of Pondicherry wrote in his diary that there were nearly 3000 blacks of African origin living in and around Pondicherry as slaves for the French governors and the French army/civil officers.

Interesting information is available on the Indian slave trade by the Dutch who had large spice plantations in Indonesia and were very active in the Cape of Good Hope. Dutch merchants took large numbers of Indians from Bengal, the Coromandel Coast and Kerala as slaves and sold them in the Cape of Good Hope. Civil/military officers and ship captains who returned to Holland after their term usually brought with them slaves from India and sold them at a good profit in the Cape of Good Hope. These slaves were used for domestic work for the European settlers as well as hard work on the farms. The slaves were invariably given Christian names but their place of origin would be indicated in the records of sales and other documents for statistical purposes. Available records indicate only about 1000 Indians taken as slaves. However historians estimate the number to be over 10,000. Reverend William Wright, a missionary in the Cape of Good Hope wrote in 1830 that all those Indians brought in were domestic servants but later made slaves. As the trade was very lucrative local agents in India were very active in supplying the human commodity to the Dutch and the Portuguese. Warren Hastings wrote in a meetings minutes on May 17 1847 "the practice of stealing children from their parents and selling them as slaves has long prevailed in the country and has greatly increased since the establishment of the English government." Individual slaves ran away due to harsh conditions and found no place to survive. Most of them were caught. They were flogged, branded and sentenced to hard labour in chains. Sexual relations between whites and Indian slaves were quite common. White settlers married Indian women and their children were accepted in European society. A mixed race had developed but they identified mostly with the white Europeans. It is believed that the Afrikaner population in South Africa has Indian ancestry.

CHAPTER 4

End of Slavery and Beginning of NEO Slavery

Abolition of slave trade was mooted in the Vienna Congress convened in 1815 by the Austrian Duke Metternich. The Congress was attended by all the major European powers that gathered to redraft the European countries after the fall of Napoleon. Proposals for abolishing slave trade were initiated. The attempt to abolish slavery was thwarted by Spain and Portugal who were then dependent on the African slaves to work in their South American colonies. As the interest of other nations except Britain was not very encouraging, the Congress left the issue to be decided by the individual nations. Britain however stood firm on abolishing slavery.

William Wilberforce of England championed the cause of the abolition of slavery. The stand taken by William was intriguing. Did he really care for human dignity irrespective of race or colour or was he keener to spread Christianity in the continents of Africa and Asia where the European domination was growing? His strong Christian faith strengthened his determination to liberate the slaves. He drowned in sorrow when he saw the Blacks brought in from Africa to London in ships being sold like commodities to the merchants for distribution to various plantations in the Caribbean and United states. London in the late 1700s was the centre for black slave trade. British ship captains reportedly purchased over 50,000 African slaves every year for selling them in the Caribbean islands. Wilberforce became a friend of William Pitt the younger who was the Prime Minister of England and pursued his goal for abolishing slavery. His struggle to abolish slave trade was a long story. He tried several times to introduce the Bill of Abolition in the Parliament. Parliamentarians in the unofficial pay roll of the big slave merchants put blocks by way of delaying the matter. The relentless efforts of William finally paid off. In 1833, the British parliament passed the bill abolishing slave trade. Slave trade was made illegal and violation was punishable as crime. William is hailed as the champion against slave trade and is thought to have inspired Abraham Lincoln, the famous president of USA, who fought a civil war to eradicate slavery.

Business is business. Business tycoons will always find a way to bypass any legislation to fulfill their ambition. Europeans particularly the British who mastered the seas around the world wanted to take full advantage of their supremacy. They saw enormous opportunities for sugar, tea, coffee, rubber, and spices in places like East Africa, Mauritius, Fiji Islands, Malaysia, Borneo, Ceylon and Caribbean islands. They were in dire need of hard manual labour to reap the wealth from the soils of these countries. William Wilberforce put a big dent on their greediness. They found a way to practice slavery in a legalized approach. This practice became known in the history of labour as Indentured Labour. Indians and Chinese were the main victims.

Literary Encyclopedia give various technical and dictionary meanings for indenture. The Webster dictionary describes it as "a contract binding one person to work for another for a given period of time"; Hutchinson's Encyclopedia explains it as 'Indentured labour was the means by which many British people emigrated to North America during the colonial days and in the 19th century. It was used to recruit Asian workers for employment elsewhere in European colonial empires". The fact is that even now it continues as a practice for the Europeans and Americans to hire the Asians, particularly Indian labour, wherever they want. Poor economic condition, oppressive social structure and frightening political situations drove many Indians to take up jobs offered by the British in the overseas colonies. British masters found the opportunity to bridge the acute labour shortage felt in the lucrative plantations in East Africa, South Africa and the Caribbean.

Labour shortage was mainly caused by the emancipated black slaves who refused to be slaves and wanted to be independent. Slave trade in the British Empire came to an end by 1834. More than half a million black slaves emancipated in the West Indies refused to continue their loyalty to their former masters. It could be due to the cruelty they underwent as slaves. In Mauritius nearly 700,000 blacks gave up their slave life and started enjoying freedom. They occupied vacant lands and started their own cultivation. Women started raising their families in a more dignified way. This new life also gave opportunities for small traders. Slowly numerous black villages sprouted out. Plantation mangers started helpless with the new situation of labour. In many companies, the blacks were demanding higher wages and the White master had no other alternative than to yield to their demands. The free slave trade practiced by British, French, Dutch and Portuguese for 200 years came to an end. This also ended the luxury enjoyed by the Europeans at the expense of the hard labour of the African blacks. Luxurious plantation products like sugar, tea, tobacco, and coffee, cotton and indigo now costed more due to the new labour situation. Heavy investments made by the Europeans, particularly the British in plantation suffered heavily. Companies were worried about the increase in cost of labour, which appreciably reduced huge profit margins. Both quality and quantity of production were coming down steadily. Price of the products rose, which in turn curtailed the demand. Sugar estates were abandoned in Jamaica, Trinidad and Mauritius. Managing plantations became a big task as well as unprofitable. Many plantations were up for sale. Estates, which were priced at $100,000 in 1810, were ready for sale for just $1500 in 1840. The situation was worsening for plantation companies particularly sugar plantation. Bankruptcy was on the increase, which alarmed the British government. Financial rescue packages were sanctioned for ailing plantation companies but it was only a short-term relief.

The British government and the companies were in serious search for an alternative arrangement. Plantation tycoons suggested hiring coolies from India and China. The situation was so critical that the government was forced to accede to the proposal. The bill permitting companies to hire indentured labour was passed in the parliament. The indentured labourer known as "coolie" was to replace the slave. A system was put in place in 1842 to hire coolies through agents in the country of origin. The word coolie is found in Chinese, Hindustani and Tamil. The meaning is hired labour. In India the word coolie refers to the porters who carry the luggages of the travelers in railway stations and seaports. Somehow the word now started denoting the unskilled Indian labour capable of only hard manual work. Now a days this word in the Caribbean, South Africa and Srilanka is considered a derogatory racial slur similar to calling an African American in USA as a Negro or Nigger.

British masters sat on the desk to calculate the cost of hiring and its sustainability. Transportation of Chinese coolies then costed double the amount of Indian coolies. Coolies from China were restricted by its labour law but this was not a big issue as the Europeans already gained enough political domination after the opium wars. The resentment of the

Chinese was overwhelming as the coolies who returned spread the news of how they were cheated, insulted and tortured by their European masters. They gained a better bargaining ground. They also demanded equal pay and treatment on par with British labour. The British also realised that discontented Chinese coolies become disorderly and even roguish. The findings and research made clear that Indian coolies were far better than the Chinese in terms of easy exploitation. The calculations also revealed that hiring Indian coolies even with high transportation cost was more economical than a local black slave who got the freedom. The Indian coolie would be very happy to have $45 per year with other amenities like bonus, food &clothing, and the option to settle down in the colony or return to India at the expense of the company after the expiry of the contract period.

Europeans also preferred Indians to the local blacks for the cleanliness and docile disposition of the Indians. When Charles Darwin visited Mauritius, he observed in his note book "Convicts from India are banished here for life; of them at present there are about eight hundred who are employed in various public works. Before seeing these people, I had no idea about the inhabitants of India were such noble looking men; their skin is extremely dark, and many of the older men had large mustachios and beards of a snow-white color; this together with fire of their expressions, gave an aspect quite imposing". Britain banished some of their hardcore criminals to far off places like Australia and British Indian officials deported a few of the Indian criminals to Mauritius for hard labour. Darwin observed that" These (Indian) convicts are generally quiet and well conducted; from their outward conduct, their cleanliness and faithful observance of their strange religious enactments, it was impossible to look at the present men with the same eyes as our wretched convicts in Australia".

The economic condition of India was quite conducive to the ambitions of the British to gather cheap labour. The British take over of Bengal and other parts of India destabilized the rural life and economy completely. The new western method of administration of lands and revenue system shattered the very basic foundation of village life. New laissez fare economy introduced by the British created different kinds of middlemen and moneylenders in the society. The land revenue was very high, which threw many small farmers out of the business. Therefore the middlemen took advantage of the British support and exploited the innocent farmers, particularly the poor and ignorant tribal people. Lands were confiscated rather grabbed mercilessly by the local zamindars or the East India Company from the farmers for non payment of taxes or the debt incurred by the farmers. Local handicraft industry was totally ruined within a period of 40 years by dumping the English and European goods at high prices. It became very common to see bonded servants who pledged their life to serve their creditor to pay off the debt. In several instances the bonded labour was extended to the descendants also. The bonded labourers were known as Kamias. Corrupt and inefficient administration of the East India Company, negligence of education and agriculture accelerated the misery of the peasant community all over India particularly where the British had direct rule. In 1836, a British official observed that "While the country in general has enjoyed peace from all external aggression, ever since it was subjected to our authority, its native inhabitants have become, every year, more and more famished" Smart and brave Kamias ran away from the clutches of their masters and reached the cities for better and honourable life. Most of them were picked up by the agents of indentured labourers. Several famines in Bihar, UP, Andhra and Central provinces occurred in short intervals driving the farmers to the cities and other parts of India. Huge labour pools were gathering in the port cities of Calcutta, Bombay and Madras where these famine stricken people took shelter. The vast availability of labour was a boon to the British who were desperately looking for workers for their plantations in Africa, Ceylon, Caribbean and Malaysia.

CHAPTER 5

Start of Plantation Coolies

Warring British and French will cooperate with each other when it is a matter of economic interest for both. Mauritius and Re union islands in the Indian Ocean were places of power struggle for both. The French was in possession of the Mauritius islands and called it as Barbourn from there they controlled the Indian Ocean trade. In 1834 the British took over the islands and brought to an end the French domination. The French already held a large area of sugar plantation in the islands. The French governors, in Pondicherry were involved in the Indian slave trade with the French plantations and the main business of one of the governors was slave trade and he barely spent time on the French political and economic activities in Pondicherry. French planters had to face the problem associated with slave labour as slavery was banned by the British throughout their empire including Asian and African colonies. French planters having invested huge amount on the sugar plantation needed British help for labourers. British was more than willing to supply the most obedient and cooperative Indian labourers from India. Slave trade was revived in the form of indentured labour, which was given legal sanction. A contract was signed between the hired labourers and the plantation owners by which the service of the labourers was made available for a fixed period. The stories of indentured labourers from India are interesting as well as humiliating.

The hiring of Indians for the Caribbean and Mauritius started almost simultaneously. The abolition of slavery in the British Caribbean in 1834 prompted the Gillanders, Arbuthnot & Company in Calcutta, a part of the East India Company, to recruit coolies from India to fill the resulting void in the labour force. The company hired Sinha, a fierce small timer who sold dreams of El Dorado to the unsuspecting, impoverished coolies. They signed a five-year contract as indentured servants. Upon arrival, the coolies were promptly enslaved by the British planters. John Scoble of the British and Foreign Anti Slavery Society arrived at the colony a year later to discover a new form of slavery; this time on the backs of Indians. Following is the letter exchanged between the coolie trader and the plantation owner.

Letter from Gladstone Esq. a estate owner in the Caribbean to Messers Gillanders, Arbuthnot & Co.

"Dear Sirs: Liverpool, 4 January 1836.

I met with an accident here about three weeks ago, which confined me to the house from which I am now recovering, and hope in few days to be able to return to Edinburgh; this will account to you for using my son's pen for writing in place of my own.

I observe by a letter which he received a few days a go from Mr. Arbethnot, that he was sending a considerable number of a certain class of Bengaless, to be employed as laboureres, to the Mauritios.

You will probably be aware that we are very particularly situated with our Negro apprentices (emancipated slaves who continue with the same masters are known as apprentices) in the west Indies, and that it is a matter of doubt and uncertainty how far they may be induced to continue their services on the plantations after their apprenticeship expires in 1840. This to us is a subject of great moment and deep interest in the colonies of Demerara and Jamica. We are therefore most desirous to obtain and introduce laboureres from other quarters, and particularly from climates something similar to their nature. Our plantation labour in the field is very light; much of it, particularly in Demerara, is done by task-work which for the day is usually completed by two o" clock in the afternoon, giving to the people all the rest of the day to themselves. They are furnished with comfortable dwellings and abundance of food; plantations, the produce of the colony, being the most common, and preferred generally by them; but they have also occasionally rice, Indian corn, meal, ship's biscuits and a regular supply of salt cod-fish, as well as the power of fishing for themselves in the trenches. They have likewise an annual allowance of clothing sufficient and suitable for the climate; there are schools on each estate for the education of the children, and the instruction of their parents in the knowledge of religious duties. Their houses are comfortable, and it may be fairly said they pass their time agreeably and happily. Marriages are encouraged and when improper conduct on the part of the people takes place, there are public stipendiary magistrates, who take cognizance of such, and judge between them and their employers. They have regular medical attendance whenever they are indisposed, at the expense of their employers. I have been particular in describing the present situation and occupation of our people, to which I ought to add, that their employment in the field is clearing the land with the hoe, and, w here required, planting fresh canes. In the works apportion are occupied in making sugar, and in the distilleries, in which they relieve each other, which makes their labor light. It is of great importance to us to endeavor to provide a portion of other laborers, whom we might use as set-off, and when the time for it comes, make us, as far as it is possible, independent of our negro population; and it has occurred to us that a moderate number of Bengalese, such as you were sending to the Isle of France (Mauritius), might be very suitable for our purpose; and on this subject I am now desirous to obtain all the information you can possibly give me. The number I should of taking and sending by one vessel direct from Calcutta to Demerara would be about 100; they ought to be young, active, able-bodied people. It would be desirable that a portion of them, at least one-half, should be married. And their wives disposed to work in the field as well as they themselves. We should require to bind them for a period not less than five years or more than seven years. They would be provided with comfortable dwellings, food, and medical assistance; they would also, if required be provided with clothing, or wages to provide themselves, which, for able bodied would not exceed four dollars per month, and in that proportion for females and their children as they grow up; a free passage would be given to them to Demerara, where they would be divided, and 20 to 30 placed on one plantation. I do not know whether the class refered to are likely to be of a particular caste, and under the influence of certain religious feelings, and also restricted to any particular kind of food; if so, we must endevour to provide for them accordingly. You will particularly oblige me by giving me, on receipt, all the information you possibly can on this interesting subject; for, should it be of an encouraging character, I should immediately engage for one of our ships to go to Calcutta, and take a limited number to Demerara, and from thence return here. On all other subjects I refer you to letter from the house; and always am,

Dear Sirs,

Yours truly

John Gladstone.

The letter from Messrs. Gillanders, Arbuthnot & Co. to John Gladstone, Esq.

"Calcutta, 6 June 1836

Dear Sir:

We beg to acknowledge your letter of the 4th January, referring to your desire to procure natives from this part of the world to work upon your estates in the West Indies, and in some degree render you independent of the Negro population at the termination of the present system; and it is with regret that at the time the letter under reply was written you were suffering from an accident, the effects of which, however, we hope ere this are entirely gone.

Within the last two years upwards of 2000 natives have been sent from this to the Mauritius, by several parties here, under contracts of engagement for five years. The contracts we believe are all of a similar nature; and we enclose copy of one, under which we have sent 700 or 800 men to the Mauritius; and we are not aware that any greater difficulty would present itself in sending men to the West Indies, the natives being perfectly ignorant of the place they agree to go to, or the length of the voyage they are undertaking. The tribe that is found to suit best in the Mauritius is from the hills to the north of Calcutta and the men of which are all well-limbed and active, without prejudice of any kind, and hardly any ideas beyond those of supplying the wants of nature, arising it would appear, however, more from want of opportunity than from any natural deficiency, of which there is no indication in their countenance, which is often one of intelligence. They are also very docile and easily managed, and appear to have no local ties, nor any objection to leave their country.

In the event of your determining to introduce these people in the West Indies and sending a ship for them, a contract such as the one enclosed, if approved, or modified or enlarged as you may think necessary, may be entered into with any number of men you would wish us to procure, and this contract upon landing the men in the West Indies and being registered at the police office would, we conclude, give your managers sufficient power to insist upon their performing any reasonable task they may be set to. Such has been the case in the Mauritius, and in one or two instances where the men have been idle or lazy, they have been punished by the competent authorities. I would perhaps avoid after-discussion were the currency in which the men will be paid, and its equivalent value with the rupee, stated in the contract. The best period for procuring and shipping the men is in our cold season, between the months of November and April, and the instruction to procure the men should precede the ship about two months, to give time to collect them; we should of course not be able to find a cargo for the ship, but some marshy rice might be sent, which with a little care would keep for three years.

The security taken by government here upon taking natives to England is to protect the East India company from loss in the event of natives being left in England without the means of subsistence or of finding their way back, in which case the Company are bound to provide for them until a passage to India can be procured, but no guarantee is required upon sending men elsewhere; as however the colonial government will probably make the importer enter into an agreement that these men shall be no burden to the colony, a provision is made in the contract to withhold so much of their allowances as will pay their passage back, should it be found necessary to discharge them before their period of service has been expired.

We fear we should not find so many as half of the number provided with wives; as, however, our friends at the Isle of France (Mauritius) speak very favorably of the men hitherto sent, many of whom our friends write to us have their task completed by two o'clock and go home leaving the Negroes in the field.

We are not aware that we can say anymore on this subject, unless we add, in inducing this men to leave their country, we firmly believe we are breaking no ties of kindred, or in any way acting a cruel part.

The hill tribes known by their name of Dhangurs are looked down upon by the more cunning natives of the plains, and they are always spoken of as more akin to the monkey than the man. They have no religion, no education, and, in their present state no wants beyond eating, drinking and sleeping; and to procure which they are willing to labour. In sending men to such a distance, it would of course be necessary to be more particular in selecting them, and some little expense would be incurred, as also some trouble; but to aid any object of interest to you, we should willingly give our best exertions in any manner likely to b of service.

We are, & c.

Gillanders, Arbuthnot & Co.

P.S. – You will observe, upon reading over the form of our contract, that it is registered in our Police-Office, and authenticated by one of the magistrates, in whose presence the document is signed, after the nature of it has been explained to the parties in their own language.

(Signed) G.,A. & Co.

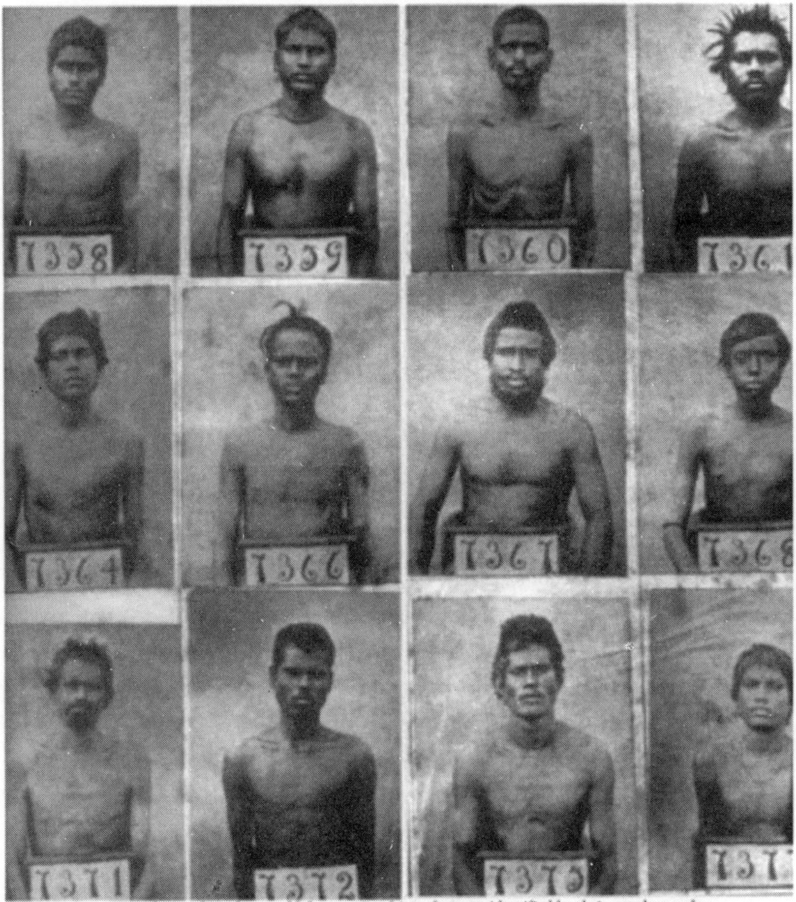

Roster of arrivals/indentured labour in S. Africa who were identified by their numbers only
(Photo Courtesy: Book titled "From Cane Fields to Freedom")

Arrival of Indian Indenture Labour in South Africa
who are identified by numbeers.

Courtesy : www.southafrica.com - book from Cane Fields to Freedom

CHAPTER 6

Coolies in the Caribbean

Indentureship to the Caribbean, the 'coolie trade' started when two ships the SS Hesperus and the SS Whitby landed in British Guiana from India on 5th May 1838. The Indian coolies were replacing the labour force of African origin.

John Scoble-Secretary of the Anti-Slavery Society alleged that the scheme "give a 'Carte blance' to every villain in British Guiana and every scoundrel in India to kidnap and inveigle into contracts over labour for five years, the ignorant and inoffensive Hindoo". The recruiters were paid according to the number they brought in. Their practices to procure men were horrifying; apart from temptation and misleading information, they also resorted to kidnapping and detaining innocents in private until they agreed to sign the contract. Indentured coolies were threatened to co operate with the agents in the event of an enquiry from government. Women, most of them widows and destitute deserted by their families or communities were also recruited. During famines women of high social status opted to emigrate rather than face starvation. Married women were lured from their husbands, daughters separated from their parents and children kidnapped. They were all registered as dependents of third persons to become eligible for the journey.

The Voyage from Calcutta to the Caribbean was not less than 4 months under normal circumstances. It could extend by one or two months under bad weather condition or hostilities due to war or piracy. More than 30% of the coolie cargo died during the voyage and another 5 to 10% within a month's time after landing. The death rate of infants was confirmed at 50% during the voyage. Reports indicate that during 1856-57 12 ship loads of 4100 Indian coolie cargo left India, out of which 700 died on the ships before completing the journey. The dead bodies were just pushed out of the deck into the sea like a bundle of garbage. The British government, strongly criticized by social pressure groups, slowly improved the condition of voyage.

More cruelties waited as soon as they landed from a horrifying journey. The English masters never adhered to the agreements regarding working condition. Working hours were unduly long, the idea of rest inconceivable; movement of labor severely restricted. Severe discipline was enforced with whips and canes flashing freely. Absence from work met with jail punishment without enquiry. Suicide by labourers unable to bear the pain of torture was very common.

Flogging in public was common and used as a means to terrorise the Indians. Influential British social activists put an end to the torture. Plantation masters countered the move by initiating the Immigration Ordinance of 1864. This ordinance compelled the master to provide housing and medical facilities to Indians. The same ordinance also included stringent restrictions on the labourers. An Indian who disobeyed his master may face fine up to $ 24 and two months imprisonment. Wages would be forfeited if he was found drunk, using foul language to his superiors. Absenteeism for more than 7 days and drifting out from work place were punishable with two months imprisonment.

Barbadian novelist George Lamming remarked, "These Indian hands whether in British Guinea or Trinidad have fed all of us. These hands were to contribute, as much as the hands of African slaves and their descedents, to the Caribbean experiment of giving shape to a unique expression of human civilization. In the words of Tinker "Indentured labour was a new form of slavery. There is, in this abominable exercise, a salutary lesson for those who have been the victims of European domination with its characteristically merciless, self aggrandizing, and malign the features, for when Europeans saw fit to bestow' freedom upon a certain people they could only do so by chaining others."

The last batch of indentured Indians arrived in 1914 and the last repatriation left Jamaica in 1929. A few left Jamaica and worked for the Panama Canal project.

Surinam is a well-known colony of the Dutch where Indian settlers are found in large numbers. Surinam changed hands several times between the British and the Dutch and finally became a Dutch colony. In the beginning, the Dutch imported indentured coolies from China to work in the sugar and coco plantations. The Dutch turned to British India for supply of indentured labour during the 1870s. Indians formed 45% of the total 80,000 indentured labours imported and the remaining was shared by Indonesians (Jawanese), China and Madeira.

Impressed by the good behavior and efficiency of the Indian labour in British Guinea, the Jamaican planters preferred Indians. Recruiting centers in Calcutta and Madras were established and the recruiters received handsome commission. They were able to lure the innocent villagers from Uttar Pradesh/Bihar skilled in agriculture. The agents assured lucrative salary, which was irresistible to the ignorant villager. The low caste villagers were more attracted as their income as well as their social status was the lowest in the society. They dreamt of beginning a new life with more income and more respect. It was a shock to those who were looking for a free and honorable life to find themselves isolated from society and stringent restrictions checked their movement. Agents were asked to target agricultural labourers. Till date, most of the Indian families who came 150 years ago still live in the rural areas and are confined to agriculture.

CHAPTER 7

Coolies in Mauritius

Indian indentured labourers to Mauritius had a slightly different story. Mauritius was a strategic place to control trade in the Indian Ocean particularly with India and Far East. Portuguese occupied the place for a brief period, later it was under the control of the French. The British snatched the islands from the French in 1810. Mauritius was a kind of take over from the French by the British. Slavery was in force during the French regime and Britain slowly abolished it and replaced it with a scheme of apprenticeship. All black slaves left the island and hence labour shortage ensued. This paved the way for the import of indentured Indian labour. The life of Indian coolies was no better than their counterparts in Caribbean. British officials spoke openly about the miserable life of Indians in Mauritius

Special Justice Anderson reported the pathetic condition of the Indians to the Governor William Nicolay in 1839. He reported that Indians are overworked, without proper shelter, deprived of adequate medical attendance, and seriously abused by the masters. He expressed his astonishment about the patience and forbearance displayed by the Indians under these miserable conditions. He added that many of the labourers had been kidnapped from their own country. They were also induced to leave their place under circumstances of fraud.

Mr. Anderson further reported that "fact is established beyond dispute, that multitudes have been kidnapped—forced into prison-depots until the Mauritian slavers were ready to receive them-hurried on board-put under hatches and guards-robbed and pillaged of the advances made to them by the Maurtian agents in Calcutta—shipped in large numbers on board vessels, without the requisite accommodation, food, or medical attendance—brought under the most fraudulent contracts to labour for years on scanty wages, and scanty fare-separated from their families and from their homes-compelled to perform the hardest agricultural labour known, at the discretion of their masters-and without the protection of an upright, impartial, and efficient magistracy."

Mr. Anderson also pointed out that the mortality rate of Indians was as high as 9% which might wipe out the Indian labour force in 10 years.

F.R. Prinsep, Secretary of the government of India reported the dubious ways of procuring labourers to colonies. He charged that the system was a source of abuse and injury rather than benefit to the labourers.

British Governor William Nicoloy confirmed the very nefarious practices prevailing in the port cities of India to procure the labourers in his letter to Lord Glenelg in 1839.

An estimated number of 750,000 indentured Indian labourers were imported from 1834 to 1920. This figure includes several hundred children, a few accompanied by their parents and a few brought in without parents. The available sample statistics of import of Indian labour Period 1834 AD to 1838 AD (An indication of geographical representation)

13243 from Calcutta (men, women and children)

308 from Cochin (males)

5058 from Pondicherry (Males)

441 from Rajahmundry (Males and females)

The plight of child labourer narrated by an aged Indian resident of Mauritius". There were many children among the recruited; some were accompanied by their parents and others, like "pardada" (from my mother's side) came alone. He was 14 and his brother who came along with him was 12. They were told by the recruiting agent in India that they were going to a land of milk and honey, they could eat as much as possible in exchange for some "light labour", but the reality was very bitter. My pardada and his brother were forced to work 7 days a week from early morning until late in the afternoon on the cane fields. Both were indentured by a sugar estate in Flacq for a period of 8 years. Many children like my pardada were brought up by the indentured community. They taught the children how to cook & wash, and be disciplined l. When pardada reached the age of 18, the sugar estate owner forced him to marry a girl of his age who was indentured by the same owner. Soon after the marriage, my grandfather Ramessar Sobrun was born and my pardada told his wife that he would return back to his homeland immediately after his contract was expired. He still had 4 years to go. Unfortunately, due to hard labour, pardada expired. Some years later his younger brother and many others died due to a cholera outbreak. Luckily grandfather Ramessar survived and grew up with the community. My mother remembers him holding her and looking into her eyes and saying, "tor ankhwa bharat ke masoom laika ke tara bah", meaning you have got the same innocent look like those children who came from India. While I was researching the archives of indentured Indians, I came across many indentured children in former British colonies and decided to travel to Bharat (India) to capture the "origin of this look".

Mauritius is now an independent country administered by the descendants of the indentured coolies. India and Mauritius have a very close relationship.

CHAPTER 8

Coolies in East Africa (Kenya/Uganda/Tanzania/Zambia/ Botswana/Zimbabwe)

India had ancient trade connections with East Africa. Our real connection started only when British colonized the eastern African countries. The British hired skilled Indians to run their administrative machinery. It was tough time of survival for Indians. They were caught between the grudging local blacks and the scorning and dictatorial whites who conquered the region.

Indians from Punjab and North Western region who generally have strong physique were hired to do the hard railway line erection. More than 30,000 Indians were brought in to build the British East African Railway from port Mombasa to Kampala the capital of Uganda. Records indicate that Indian workers died four per every mile of the railroad while building. Their life was mostly fraught with danger. Stories are still in the air that lions roaming in the jungle had their feasts on the flesh of Indians who lost their way during their work in the railway project running across the jungles. A movie was made in 1966 based on these incidents tilted "The Ghost and the

Darkness". Gujarathis were encouraged by the British to start small business like grocery shops to bring in Indian articles for the use and consumption of Indian workers. As the blacks were totally backward in trade and commerce (even now the same situation prevails in many parts of East Africa) the supply and distribution work was done by the Indian Gujarathis.

Gujarathis and Marwadies, who are born traders, found the place like a free hunting ground as there were no rules and regulations to start business and conduct it the way they wanted to. The British political protection kept them safe against the natives who grudged the relatively better life of Indian traders. Kenya was probably the only east African country which had made progress under the control of British. Uganda, Zambia and Tanzania did not develop like Kenya. The British domination in these countries, however, remained strong which helped many Gujarathi businessmen to start business and flourish under a totally free economy.

When these countries became independent Africanisation was unleashed by the leaders. Their target was to prune the Indian traders who had no political support either from India or Britain. Africans had been grudging that the entire retail business was in the hands of Indians. Indians never mingled with Africans nor did they participate in the freedom struggle of the nations where they lived and became rich. Indians had their affinity with India and allegiance to the queen of Britain. Idi Amin gave 3 months to the Indians to leave the country when he made the anti Indian drive and majority of the Ugandan Indians moved to Britain, Canada and USA. A few found jobs in the Middle East and moved to places like Bahrain, Kuwait and UAE. Many Goans from Kenya and Uganda migrated after the Africanisation drive during the early 1970s. Very few chose to come back to India, not for settlement but to stay until they found a job abroad. Britain kept its promise to safeguard their interest and provided many with a British passport which was preferred by almost all. The independent African states felt the hard pinch of the absence of Indian traders and professionals immediately after evicting them. New leaders who came to power through overthrow or by rebellion invited back the Indians. Many returned but with British passports which ensured better protection. Rich Indians in Uganda, Zambia and Kenya still keep their British passport and pay allegiance to Her Majesty the Queen of Britain.

Botswana and Zimbabwe started attracting Indian labour much later. Both the countries although very rich, could afford to keep qualified Indian labour. Many white collar jobs like doctors, accountants, professors, engineers are till date efficiently handled by Indians. These countries have sizeable Indian communities.

Arrival of Indentured Indians

Arrival of Indentured Indians

The Natal Mercury.

THURSDAY, NOVEMBER 22, 1860.

THE COOLIES HERE.

The past week will long be memorable amongst Anglo-Natalians. At last, after the discussion of years and the extinction of hopes innumerable, the planters' pet project has been realised. There has been so much said in certain quarters against the immigration of Coolies, as a piece of

(English Daily in Natal)

CHAPTER 9

Coolies in South Africa

South Africa is a land of immense natural resources like diamond mines, gold mines and fertile agricultural lands. Power struggle between the Boers (Dutch settlers) and the British went on for several years. Germany also carved a portion (Namibia) in the south west of South Africa as its colony. The local Zulus gave considerable problems to the white settlers from Europe. Finally it became a large country administered by both the Dutch and British with Britain in the political driver seat. South Africa imported large numbers of indentured labour from India. Immediately after the abolition of slavery in 1833, South Africa also felt the dire need for hard labour. The blacks who were so frustrated with the treatment by their masters decided not to work with their White masters.

The first batch of Indian coolies numbering 380 arrived on 16th November 1860 by SS Truro at the port of Durban. The arrival of Indian indentured labour was described as shipment of human or coolie cargo. More than 60% of the 152000 who arrived in South Africa from 1860 to 1911 were from Madras presidency and Coromandel Coast (Andhra Pradesh, Orrisa and Bengal). Indian labourers were hired by the sugar plantations owned by the British and Dutch. The initial labour contract was a period of 5 years and they were tempted with an extension of another 5 years. Contracts stipulated that at the end of the contract they will be shipped back to India at the company's cost or lands would be given with option to stay in South Africa. The harsh labour in South Africa was no better than other colonies. Work was extracted from dawn to dusk with no weekly holiday. They were put up in crowded shabby barracks and the rations were meager and of poor quality. Indians in excess of garden requirements were disbursed to other areas of works like mines, railways, shipyards and domestic works for the Europeans. South African whites openly admitted that the economy of Natal province had improved considerably due to the hard work of the Indians.

Another wave of Indians arrived in South Africa during the early 1900s and they were known as "passenger Indians". They were mostly the trading community from Gujarath who found South Africa a hunting ground for retail trading. They entered Natal and Transvaal and rapidly expanded their retail operation. The apartheid administration of SA wanted to have the cake and eat it too. They were annoyed by the growing prosperity of the indentured Indians after 50 years. Many laws and legislations were passed to curb the influx of the Indians and also to discourage them to venture into business by imposing high level of taxes. The White business community however wanted the cheap, dedicated and cooperative Indian labour. In 1911 Gopalakrishna Gokhale cried out in the Legislative Council deploring the cunning way Indians were being lured into South Africa by local agents and also the sub human life of Indians at the hands of white Europeans. The South African government put an end to the indenture trade and tried to push many Indians out by implementing harsh and insulting laws against Indians. Despite the hard conditions and apartheid insults 75% of Indians remained in South Africa.

Indians did not get along well with the black locals although both were exploited by the whites. Indians, being foreigners normally behaved well and more co operative with their masters. Higher education level was another plus point against the blacks. Indians were generally placed as number two in the administration which generated hatred towards the Indians. They were like sub masters which was very hard for the local blacks to digest. The two slave communities never got together socially even after living side by side for over a century. It is very surprising that reportedly, considerable percentage of Indians prefer the apartheid regime in the place of the free country where the African National Congress with blacks forming the majority runs the administration. They attributed this to the high rate of crime in the country that erupted after the end of Whites only regimes and as a result the normal daily life of citizens in many parts of the country has become stressful.

It is possible that a few decades down the road, the majority of the whites may emigrate to Australia and/or USA. Where will the Indians go if they are unable to bear the tough and uncompromising government of the blacks? Many Indians might have already chalked out a future plan to move to USA or Canada and a negligible percentage would prefer to return to India.

CHAPTER 10

Coolies in South East Asia (Burma/Fiji Islands/Singapore/ Malaysia/Sri Lanka)

Burma (Mynmar)

Indian merchants and Brahmanas exercised great influence in the social and economic life of Burmese since the 7th century. Buddhism was spread by the Indians. The real migration of Indians started after the Anglo Burmese war, through this war country was brought under the control of the British crown.

The British took the Indians as coolies even to the East Asian countries where they had established their control or dominance. They subdued the Burmese in 40 years time starting from 1856 to 1896 AD with the help of Indian soldiers. By 1890 AD Burma was totally under the control of the British. It is to be noted by all Indians that the resentment of Burmese to accept British rule was unanimous and they openly refused to cooperate with them although they were conquerors. The British found it very difficult to introduce their way of administration and systems which they effortlessly implemented in India. Britain did not want to give up the vast natural resources available in Burma. Their experience with submissive Indians helped them to achieve their goal in Burma. Many Indians from the east coast starting from Bengal to Kanyakumari were recruited or encouraged to take up assignments in Burma. It was a craze to find the way to Burma during 1900 to 1930 for better prospects. It was like the Gulf craze of the 1970s and 80s. Large numbers of Indians were recruited in railways, post and telegraphs, customs and government departments. Timber and oil companies run by the British hired Indians to administer their business. Indian inflow started swelling to the great wrath of the local Burmese year by year. All the government jobs were occupied by Indians. The merchant community from Tamilnadu called Chettiars found a lucrative business of money lending to the Burmese peasants. Hundreds of Tamilians and Telugus found good paying jobs in the government and private companies owned by the British. The Chettiars were well protected by the colonial laws. Retail trade was in the hands of Indians. There is a leather shop at Luz corner in Chennai city which till date displays its board as an establishment registered in Rangoon in 1919 AD. The anti foreigner feeling was growing not only against the British but also against the imported Indians. The labour and peasants unrest reached its peak in 1930 when the movement "Do Bama" (Burma for Burmese) erupted against all foreigners particularly Indians. The 1930 revolt targeted Indian shops and households. Indians started leaving the country and the plight of Indians sufferings in Burma is an age old story in Tamilnadu. The revolt was suppressed by a military force consisting of soldiers from Punjab. In 1937 AD, Burma was separated from India. During the 2nd World War the British were driven out of Burma by the Japanese forces. As the British protection disappeared many Indians fled Burma and came to India. The Indian population of one million reduced to 500,000 in a matter of 2 years from 1941 to 1943.

During the period from 5th to 12th century Indian culture, education, religion and philosophy was admired by the

Burmese. Red carpet welcome was given to scholars from India who preached Buddhism and engineers and craftsmen who worked as consultants for the constructions of various Buddhist monasteries like the famous Swazigon Pagodas near Rangoon. In 1930 thousands of Indians were driven out of the land as they were looked down upon as stooges of the British. The Burmese did not like Indians as they helped the British not only to conquer their country but also exploit their natural resources. Burmese, even now refuse to acknowledge the cultural and geographical proximity with India and lean more towards China, It may be due to their hatred towards Indian soldiers. India's generous gesture of writing off debts owed by Burma to India immediately after independence from British rule was also not accepted in good spirit and gratitude.

Around 300,000 still live in independent Burma. Indian schools, cultural societies, temples and churches exclusively for south Indians still exist.

Fiji Islands

A country which was feared as a land of cannibals was explored by the Dutch and the British in the early 18th century. The British took control of the islands and found vast potential for sugar and cotton. The local population was very thin and utterly backward rather tribal with no civilization. Britain had always been lucky to have had Indians under its thumb. India was a mine of cheap labourers of different skills. Leonidas was the name of the ship that carried the first batch of 460 Indians to Fiji. Britain appointed Sir Arthur Gordon as the Governor who had prior experience in managing plantations and Indian labour. He was considered an expert in managing Indians. The same procedure of signing papers to be hired as labour with standard terms and conditions used for sending coolies to Caribbean was followed. The papers which they signed before coming to Fiji were called GIRMIT meaning agreement. The National museum in Australia still has the original copies of the 60,000 entry permits issued to the indentured Indians since 1879 to 1916. Indian labourers were sheltered in a shed like cattle. It was compulsory to work for a minimum period of 5 years and they became eligible to get ticket back to India only after 10 years of work. The yoke of the agreement was released after 5 years and the Indians were given option to continue or develop a piece of land given to them. Indians by virtue of their higher educational standards could find government jobs. Small shops selling Indians goods were started by Gujarathies. As usual the Indians did not mingle with the local Fijians; here also they were cast between the ignorant locals and the clever colonial masters. The locals hated them while the British exploited them. Indenturing was stopped in 1916 and the 60,000 strong Indian labourers were already in a dominant position in the government and business. The British were skeptical about Indians taking over the islands after their departure therefore played the same divide and rule game. They injected hatred in the minds of the local Fijians and encouraged an anti Indian campaign. The cry "Fiji for Fijians" by the locals was the same as the cry of Burmese "Burma for Burmese". Indians were made the scapegoat in the struggle for independence.

When Fiji became independent, local Fijians had no other alternative than to relay on the administrative skills of the Indians who got naturalized as Fijians. Fiji is one of the few countries (Mauritius, Surinam) where descendants of the indentured Indians took over the government after the departure of the British.

Malaysia, Singapore and Sri Lanka

Malaysia, Singapore and Sri Lanka had cultural, trade and religious connections with India for several centuries. The cultural domination of India over Malaysia (Kedha), Singapore and Sri Lanka (Elangai or Elam) dates back to 600 AD (6th century). Trade between India and China was routed through these countries. The Malaysian and Singapore connections got cut off after the invasion of Mongols in the 13th century. Indian Muslims played a key role in Islamisation of Malaysia and Indonesia where the Hindu and Buddhists religions were predominant for several centuries. These countries were controlled by the Dutch for a century before they were colonized by Britain in the 1800s.

The British quickly realized the great economic potential in the region. Tea, rubber, sugar and coffee plantations were developed. As usual they brought in Indian coolies particularly from Tamilnadu and the Coromandel Coast to develop the plantations and tin mining. KANKANIS (labour broker) were hired by the master to tempt and cajole the innocent and impoverished agricultural peasants. Kankanis were ruthless in their job and got commission from both sides. Drought in 1860 swept through the Madras presidency and put thousands of farmers out of job. Finding no other alternative, many were ready to go to far off places by selling or pledging their valuables to find placements (!) arranged by the Kankanis. Kankani became a notorious word in Tamil Nadu and Andhra for describing high level of selfishness and unreliability. Nagapatnam, a port near Tanjore was the embarking place for Tamilians. The import of Indian coolies started from 1860 and by the end of 1930 there were 450,000 Indian indentured labourers in Malaysia. Singapore was developed as a strategic commercial port and the Indian merchants were encouraged to start small businesses. Indian convicts were used for hard labour and 2 battalions of Madras Regiment were stationed to give military protection.

The Malaysian peninsula and the adjoining regions developed very fast giving great opportunities for the shipping business. Hundreds of Indians entered these two countries illegally in the beginning of 1900s. The rubber industry in Malaysia had 300,000 Indian labours which was almost 60% of the total labour force employed. By 1940, the Indian population crossed 500,000 i.e. 15% of the total population. Tamil became one of the official languages besides English, Chinese and Malay. During the Second World War, thousands of Indians fought against the invading Japanese to protect the British crown (Singapore was a crown colony directly under the British crown). As Singapore was becoming a great commercial port, most of the administrative positions were taken by the English knowing Indians. Malaysia and Singapore became independent countries in the 1960s. The plantations were still controlled by the British companies which employed thousands of Indians. Those Indians who made money and wanted to settle down in India returned back, but a sizable number remained in the peninsula and became permanent residents. The reluctance of Indians mingling with local Malaysians created a cultural gap; however no major conflict between the two communities took place either before or after independence.

Sri Lanka was another lucrative discovery of the British for exploitation. Coffee and tea plantations were developed during the 1870s when the island was brought under British control. Thomas Lipton was the famous planter merchant who made a big fortune in tea. More than 1.5 million Tamil workers were brought into Sri Lanka within a period of 75 years to develop plantations. Tamil population remained in Sri Lanka even after its independence from Britain in 1950. Tamil population which is 7% of the total is now facing the wrath of the ethnic Sri Lankans. Tamils were looked down upon as coolie immigrants disregarding the fact that the link between Tamil Nadu and Sri Lanka was as old as the Saiva cult that flourished for 9th centuries in Sri Lanka much before the advent of Europeans in the 1700s.

During the 8th and 9th centuries (800AD, 900AD) Indians from Tamil Nadu went to Malaysia, Singapore and Sri Lanka as conquerors. Rajendhra Chola of Tanjore raided the Javanese kingdom of Sri Vijaya and brought under his control the Java region including places now known as Singapore, Java and Malaysia. Raja Raja Chola (Father of Rajendra Chola) conquered almost the entire Sri Lanka and the Cholas ruled over it for a century. The Chola soldiers could possibly have embarked from Puhar, a port town in the Chola kingdom to subdue the Malaysian peninsula and Sri Lankan island. Nagapatnam not far from Puhar, in 19th century, became an embarking port for the indentured Indian labourers (mostly Tamils) who were shipped to Malaysia, Sri Lanka and Singapore to work as garden coolies in the rubber, sugar and tea plantations. What a cruel fate!

CHAPTER 11

Coolies in Australia and New Zealand

Australia and New Zealand treated the Indians relatively better. This may be because of the white racial policy adopted by both. The whites only policy (White Australian policy) was open in Australia but New Zealanders followed it in the initial stages as a practice but did not pursue it as a national policy. The policy made the world know that only white race will have the opportunities and rights of the unexplored continent.

It is believed that the ship of Captain Cook who discovered Australia and New Zealand had Indian lascars. When development began in the continent, many Indians from Kabul and Punjab were imported as camel drivers. They carried goods and mail on the camel back from the interior to the port cities. They were used to maintain the communication and supply line between Melbourne and interior Australia. The weather and terrain of central Australia which is mostly a desert was very suitable to Indians. Indians were easily picked up by the British and European settlers as both Australia and India were part of the British Empire. Sikhs from Punjab were brought into work in the banana plantations in southern Queensland. Over the years, the Sikhs became owners of the plantations. Wolgoolga is a town in the highway between

Sydney and Brisbane where the Sikhs live in large numbers. Australia was very reluctant to bring in Indians and Chinese as they feared that their population will increase over the years and might precipitate a social and ethnic problem like South Africa and Malaysia. There was not much of a rush to Australia like the Caribbean and Africa.

The Whitlam labour government in 1972 abolished the white race policy and opened the country for Asians and Africans. They found the country facing a negative population growth due to the slow progress of economy. This new opening brought in many Fiji Indians, Gujarathi, Sindhi and Bengali traders from India. The recent influxes of Indians are the students. Australian universities are starving for funds as the government financial support is receding. They look for overseas students, particularly from India. As India has also liberalized its foreign exchange policy and foreign educational studies with bank loans, it has become very common in English newspapers to see Australian universities advertising opportunities for higher education to Indian students in Australia. Indian students are tempted by the prospect of a decent and paying job in Australia itself after finishing their studies. The Indian population, which was hardly 7500 in 1947, is now reaching the 100,000 mark.

New Zealand, a thinly populated British controlled (Dominion) country in the south Pacific did not have a harsh history of Indentured Indians. In the beginning only men who made their living by running petty shops, as hawkers, bottle and garbage collectors, gardeners and kitchen cleaners were imported. New Zealand railway hired few Indians for building tracks and also to drain and clean swamps. The White population was very thin and there was a fear that Indians might outnumber them if a liberal policy was adopted. This led to the formation of an anti Indian league, which cried "Keep New Zealand a White man's Country". South African type of racism was prevalent in few places of New Zealand until the First World War. New Zealand opened its gates from 1980 removing all kinds of discrimination. Indians here are mostly from Gujarath and Punjab region. The present strength is around 75,000. The second generation Indians and those who migrated from Fiji are now leading a respectable life as New Zealanders engaged in business and in dignified professions like healthcare, education, sports and arts.

CHAPTER 12

Coolies in Western World (Europe, USA and Canada)

Europe

Racial discrimination and language barrier are the two factors, which discouraged Indians in continental Europe. Indians form a minute minority in European countries except Britain. Britain was the only country in Europe that harboured Indians from different parts of the country due to their colonization of India. After the independence both Pakistanis and Indians from the respective Punjab region were recruited as industrial labourers. Britain lost a sizable number of its youngsters in the World War, which created an acute shortage of labour for its industries. There was no exodus of workers from India due to strict governmental blockades. Pakistan and Bangladesh (previously East Pakistan) were more relaxed in sending their work force to Europe; in fact the government itself encouraged both legal and illegal emigration to foreign countries. Bradford was then the well-known place for Indians and Pakistanis. In recent years thousands of (around 22000) Indian IT professionals have entered Britain. This is in addition to the hundreds of students who have arrived for higher studies. Statistics indicate that

Britain had issued over 300,000 visas to Indians in the year 2005.

Britain became the second home for Indians immediately after independence. Indians are well off in many parts of Britain. Few Indians are wealthy and influential businessmen; a few are active politicians even attained lordships and sit in the House of Lords.

USA

The story of Indian immigration into USA and Canada is another interesting story. Reports indicate that the first batch of Indians arrived in USA 1790 AD as maritime workers. There were less than 600 Indians in USA until 1900. A few historians feel that hiring of Indians by US was hampered by the British. They, as rulers of India wanted Indians for their colonies. Indians reached the Caribbean, which is very close to USA but never, entered USA. White Americans turned their attention to Africa, China, Japan and Philippines. The main workforce, the blacks were either smuggled or forcibly traded into USA. Indians were hired in the beginning of the 20th century as labourers in saw mills, rail road maintenance and farms and they were known as "Cheap Oriental Labour". All Indians were referred to as Hindus. The Sikhs from Punjab arrived in California in 1906 and it was the beginning of the Indian entry into USA. An anti Indian riot broke out in Bellingham (State of Washington) known as "Anti-Hindu Riot" in 1907 as the local Americans were upset about their job opportunities being grabbed by the Indians. The American government was very skeptical about giving immigrant status to Indians. A Congressman in 1908 openly charged, "Indians are weak rice eaters and worshippers of different gods. They are not fit to be citizens of this tough country". The labour shortage after the Second World War forced US government to reexamine their stand against Indians. In 1946 congressmen Emmanuel Cellar and Clare Booth took initiatives that helped The Indians to seek naturalization. They sponsored the Indian Citizenship Bill which specified an annual quota of 100 Indians. The quota has gradually increased since 1952.

USA is fast emerging as the second home for the technically qualified educated Indians. Over the last 5 decades the number had risen over 1.7 million and they are now the third minority community in the country. An ethnic community known as Indian Americans had emerged. They are now respected as one of the highly educated community in USA. The achievements of Indians in business, teaching, technology and medicine are laudable. USA has produced two Noble laureates of Indian origin. The contribution of Indians in the recent technological wave is so substantial that it has created new section of billionaires like Bill Gates and Larry Ellison in USA. The Top brass like CEOs, COOs and CFOs in big established corporations like Mekinzy, Citicorp, and Hartford Financials are occupied by Indian Americans. It seems that there is no technology firm in US without an Indian. The annual buying power of Indian Americans is estimated around US $ 20 billion.

Statistics of Indian Americans. (NRILinks.com-USA)

They own 30% of hotels and motels in USA.

50% have their own homes.

65% hold managerial/professional/technical jobs.

80% have college degrees.

90% live in urban areas.

100% of those surveyed are proud of their heritage.

The average annual household income of Indian American is $88,000 compared to the average American income of $ 55,000.

The above information will make every Indian very proud. But let us look at it from a different angle. A historian remarked, "Had the blacks who worked hard to make America a wealthy nation done the same in their own native countries

Africa would have been much wealthier than what it is now". Does this statement hold good for Indians also?

Canada

Canada, despite being a British suzerainty, did not attract Indian labour. It may be due to the extreme cold climate. The first Indians who visited Canada were Sikh soldiers of the British Indian army in 1897. The Sikhs in Hong Kong started exploring opportunities in Canada. Indians are known as "Hindus" or "East Indians". British Columbia was the arrival point for Sikhs. The European settlers did not like the Indians. They did not arrive in Canada as indentured labor like in South Africa and the Caribbean but as free immigrants. Their slow and steady growth both in number and prosperity became an eye sore to the European settlers. In 1908 under heavy pressure from the European Canadians British officials planned to evict "Hindus" by offering them the option to migrate to British Honduras. The Interior Minister of the Federal Government J.B. Harken was authorized to make arrangements for the East Indians numbering 3000 to settle in British Honduras. A congregation held in Sikh temple attended by Sikhs, Hindus and Muslims rejected the proposal for a transfer to Honduras. The Canadian government offered an attractive financial package with a pension plan to relocate them but met with failure.

It was strange that the white population in Canada was ready to admit Chinese and Japanese but not the Indians. It was purely a racial animosity. Pressure had been exerted on the government to evict the Indians. The Japanese ship, (Komagata Maru) which carried 400 Sikhs from India, was not allowed in the harbor, a stiff resistance was shown by the whites to permit the Indians into the city of Vancouver. They chuckled at Indians as "The Brown Invasion". Several anti Indian activities erupted. The matter became sticky to British when the First World War broke out. The British Indian army had mostly men from Punjab and Rajasthan. The news of anti Indian (Sikh) hatred, which had reached India, could have had repercussion on the recruitment of men for the world war. The British, citing the problem, played down the anti Indian feelings in British Columbia. British Columbia is now the major centre for Punjabis particularly Sikhs. They have now become the part of the upper middle class and run most of the retail outlets particularly automobile spares in the state.

The eastern coast of Canada did not have Indians until 1950. Canada opened up its eastern gates to attract Indian engineers and doctors. The immigration laws were relaxed in 1985, which attracted the educated not only from India but also from other parts of the world. During the 1990s, hundreds of NRIs in Middle East and Far East took advantage of the relaxed immigration laws and obtained immigrant visas. Toronto city is now the centre (Mississauga) for emigrated Indians, Bangala deshis, Sri Lankans and Pakistanis.

According to many historians indentured Indian and Chinese labour were exploited by the dominating west to their economic advantages. It is very true but it also has its positive side. Here is a view expressed by a European.

Following is an interesting and thought provoking view from an European's angle.

Quote

"About three generations ago, Professor Lilian Knowles in her seminal three volume study entitled The Economic Development of the British Overseas Empire, noted the academic neglect which East Indian immigration to the western hemisphere as a historical phenomenon had received among historians. She was quick to point out in 1924 that, "It is often not sufficiently recognized that there have been two great colonizing movements in the nineteenth century. The movement of Europeans to fill up the manless lands of the New World has been largely advertised. But the importance

Returned Passengers from Vancouver a board the Komagata Maru in Budge-Budge Harbor.
(Source: Punjab and Sind Bank Calendar for 1989.)

Courtsey : punjabonline.com

of this migration of Chinese and Indian emigrants who have created new colonial values, made whole regions of the British Tropics into paying assets, and created within the British Empire a new Indian Empire in the British West Indies and a new Chinese Empire in the British Straits Settlements, has scarcely yet been recognized." (EAST INDIANS IN CANADA'S PACIFIC COAST1900-1914 AN ENCOUNTER IN RACE RELATIONS by Sahadeo Basdeo)

Unquote

There is a lot of truth in the opinion. Singapore, the advanced and wealthy city state is now governed by Chinese but is not part of China. Similarly Fiji Islands, Surinam and Mauritius are governed by Indians but are not part of India. They are all inherited from the British Empire.

CHAPTER 13

Indian Lascars

The word Lascar was derived from the Persian word "Lashkar" meaning a sailor or soldier. Indians played the role of lascars in many European ships. They were like coolies who did the odd jobs like cleaning, cooking and lifting cargos. Indians were not the only lascars in the European merchant navy; there were Chinese and Malaysians and Indonesians. Hiring Indian lascars started way back from the early arrival of Vasco Da Gama. The Portuguese used the lascars followed later by the British and the French. Many young men from Goa and the Malabar Coast were recruited and sent to European ships to work as lascars. Britain had strict rules since 1660 AD to restrict foreign nationals to be engaged in shipping, particularly in the European waters (west of Cape of Good Hope)! Despite the rules British merchant navy and naval force used Indian lascars more and more defying the rules whenever possible. The cost of English sailors was 5 times higher than Indian lascars. Further, many English sailors died due to heat and change to tropical climate whenever they traveled to India and the Far East. During the Napoleonic war, Britain lost many of its English sailors in the naval battles. The shortage of European sailors led to the mass recruitment of Asians, particularly

Indian lascars.

Lascars were recruited in gangs by a labour agent called the Ghat Serang. He was not only an agent but also a lodging housekeeper and moneylender. He bargained separately with the labourers as well as with the shipping companies. He was made responsible for the welfare of the seamen and their discipline. He had tremedous influence over the seamen who were generally poor and illiterate. Many a time the bargains were manipulated by the agent and shipping company to their advantage leaving the poor lascar with a mere pittance. Warren Hastings, the Governor General of India tried to bring regulation to safeguard the interest of the ignorant lascars. Registration office was established and wages were fixed and paid directly to the sailors cutting out the middlemen (Ghat Serangs). The Ghat Serangs who were losing by the new regulations did everything to make the new regulation ineffective.

The East India Company, which recruited the lascars for European voyages, simply abandoned them in London. They were hired back in the ship only when it sailed back to India, a normal gap of at least 3 months. Many were roaming the streets of London and a few were begging to make their living. Many resorted to drinking and use of ganja. Harassments, insults and even physical attacks by the local English on the roaming lascars were common. The life of deserted lascars was worse than black slaves. Churches and Missionary societies provided food and shelter to them. The British government in order to put an end to the destitute seamen brought a rule by which the East India Company was made responsible for their upkeep in England.

The poor and unhealthy living condition of the lascars in London and other English port cities was criticised by social activists, Christian missionaries and Parliamentarians. Indian lascars were like destitute. Recommendations and regulations to give them better living condition were grossly ignored by the shipping companies.

The service of Indian lascars continued even after independence as they were more cost effective to the shipping companies when compared to the European seamen. An issue was raised by the competing Europeans to increase the salary of Indians so that they would be on par with them. Despite government backing, the issue was not successful. Many shipping companies even now prefer Indians and Chinese as they have become acclamatised to differing weather conditions. Lascars still continue in the western merchant navy but with different dignified name like seaman or naval assistant.

There are unconfirmed reports that Israel hired Indians to work as lascars in their army and navy. The hiring process was done through the back door method. Indians would be shipped to neighbouring India friendly countries like Lebanon, Cypress and Malta; from there they would be picked up by the Israeli agents without official visa in the passport. A signed document is issued to enter and work in Israel which would be taken back when they exited. There will not be any entry in the passport for having visited and worked in Israel.

Friday afternoon, start of May 1890

A British steam ship is coming into the Royal Victoria Dock with a cargo of tea from India. Lascars work in the engine room putting coal into the boiler to fuel the ship.

Lascar 1

I'm a Lascar. A Lascar is what the British call an Asian sailor. I'm from Bengal in India and I've worked on British ships since I was 16. My father and uncles did too. They told us such great stories about their travels and about London and Queen Victoria, who is also the Empress of India.

Courtesy : timepiretes.com lessons for children about lascars

Lascar 2

Last time I came to London I had to wait for 5 months before my ship was ready to return to Calcutta. My wages didn't last long and I had to beg on the streets and sleep rough. But now I'm earning extra money working in the engine room and I'm going to leave the ship and stay and set up a shop in London

Lascar 3

They say Lascars are used to the heat so can work in the engine room, but I have never known heat like this. So many people want to work on the ships it's hard to get a job. I had to bribe the Ghat Serang, who finds jobs for sailors on ships, to let me onboard.

Courtesy : timepiretes.com lessons for children about lascars

Boiler

Lascars working in the engine room were called Ag-walla, which means fireman. Ag-wallas were paid more than other Lascars because it was a hard job. For four hours at a time they loaded coal into the boiler to power the steam ship. Many men died from heat exhaustion. European sailors were paid 4 or 5 times more than Lascars.

British Ship Engineer

Lascars are very hard working. We employ lots of Lascars on this ship as sailors, cooks and to work in the engine room. Britain rules many countries so sailors and goods are sent to London. In the docks we'll see sailors from China, Africa and Jamaica and of course lots of English dockers unloading the cargoes.

Courtesy : timepiretes.com lessons for children about lascars

CHAPTER 14

Indian Ayahs (Maid Servant) and Nurses

Indian ayahs reached England way back in 1628 AD. The parish records and gravestones in churchyard stand proof of the ayah's arrival in England. Indian ayahs were generally taken by the British and French officers who left for their country after having served in India for some time. They trusted them and liked their innocence and hard work. It was also a prestige to the rich Indian – returned British "Nabobs", to bring in Indian ayahs and domestic boys to England to take care of the needs of their family members". In a few cases, the returning English families cleverly used ayahs during the strenuous 5 months voyage from Bombay to London and their employers left them out in the city of London. It was not un common to see Indian ayahs and domestic boys begging in the streets of London when their masters deserted them. The East India Company was accused of this in human act, which made them to promulgate a regulation by which the English masters were required to sign a bond of 50 pounds to support the deserted ayahs' livelihood and return passage to India.

There was no legal protection or safe guard for them. They were like chattels of their masters. Advertisements were put on the newspapers about the availability of the ayahs and boys for domestic service. This was very close to buying and selling them in public. An advertisement in Steele's and Addison's Tatler in 1709 read: 'A black Indian Boy 12 Years of Age, fit to wait on a Gentleman, to be disposed of at Denis's Coffee-house in Finch Lane near the Royal Exchange.'

Recently reports were released about the miserable conditions of Indian Ayahs who were brought in by westerners as well as affluent Indians. Hiring of Indian Ayahs by Europeans ended after the 2nd World War.

Ayahs started going abroad again during the Gulf boom. Arabs who became rich during the 1980s due to oil boom started looking for Indian Muslim women to serve as ayahs. There were several complaints brought to the attention of the Indian embassy about how these ayahs were chased by the male members or ill treated by female members of the family. In a few countries the Indian government implemented the rule that a financial guarantee (similar to the 50.00 pounds bond introduced by East India Company) must be provided by the employers who wished to hire domestic servants (Ayahs). There were hardly any instances of ayahs being deserted by their masters and left on the streets, as it would attract the wrath of the religious priests. Unfortunately there are no meeting places for the Indian Ayahs in any of the Gulf countries, as they did not enjoy weekly holidays unlike the Philipino domestic servants working in Hong Kong. They were not allowed to go out alone or meet their fellow countrymen or women. A few suicides due to excessive oppression and frustration were also reported. They were totally under the mercy of their masters. It is a fact that despite the cruelties unleashed on them the craze among under educated Indian women to go to Gulf, as Ayahs had not receded. Most of the Ayahs are lured by the various cosmetics and fancy article available at cheap and affordable prices, much beyond their means in India. Possession of gold jewelry is a dream of almost every woman in India. Ayahs with their savings could afford to buy gold armaments. Even today it is very difficult to expose the plight of the ayahs in Gulf countries as their miseries and problems are all handled by the police and embassy officials without any involvement of the media so as to paint a rosy picture of the government and the local people.

Cheaper ayahs from Sri Lanka and Indonesia are now replacing Indian Ayahs in Arab countries.

Nurses

There is no authentic information about Indian nurses' involvement in the world wars. However the estimate could be around 5000. The demand for Indian nurses started after the Second World War Britain was the main importer of Indian nurses. Indian nurses were preferred because of their ability to communicate in English. Christian missionaries supplied trained Indian nurses to various hospitals in Europe. Gulf countries imported hundreds of Indian nurses during the boom period from 1975 to 1990. There is keen competition between the Philippinos and Indians in Gulf countries. There are around 60,000 Indian nurses working in Middle East. The reputation of Indian nurses spread to USA which eventually became the biggest importer. The demand for trained nurses in USA is on the increase. The current shortage (2005 AD) is around 130,000 and the figure is likely to cross the 400,000 mark in the next ten years. Recruitment and placement agencies have started working full time to meet the demand of USA. In the last one year, nurse training schools and institutes have mushroomed in Kerala, Karnataka, Punjab and Tamilnadu. Thousands are undergoing training to get the certificates in CGFNS (Commission of graduates of foreign nursing school). Certificates in language proficiency like TOEFL (Test for English as foreign language), TWE (Test for Written English) and TSE (Test for Spoken English) are the next step to gain entry into USA. Training institutes are signing MOUs

(Memorandum of Understanding) with hospitals in USA for supply of nurses. Aging population in USA is on the increase and the government takes care of the aged with good medical facilities. The US government had even relaxed some of the strict labor regulations to facilitate import of Indian nurses so that they reach USA without bureaucratic hassles. Nursing had replaced the demand for software engineers and it is believed that nurses get green card much easier than technology experts. The news of the easy way of getting green card had lured many qualified students including male students to seek admission in the training of nurses. This situation is similar to that of brilliant engineering students taking up computer courses, which pave a way for a jump outside India instead of, sophisticated and knowledge based civil/electrical/ mechanical/chemical studies. Training institutes have been steadily increasing their fees as much as Rs. 12000 per month as the demand is rising day by day. Nursing which was considered as a dedicated noble profession and confined to missionaries is now commercialized fetching good income for the recruitment agencies.

Are Indian nurses in the hospitals treated with honour or they are like any garden coolie of the last century? There are reports of racial harassment present in many hospitals. This however did not develop into a major problem but the Indian nurses feel that they are being treated as inferior to the whites. Indian nurses forget that they had arrived to make their living on a scale better than what they would have got in India. As usual Indian nurses enjoy the reputation for efficiency and obedience and are preferred over competing Philipino nurses.

While India is enthusiastic to provide as many trained nurses as possible for USA and Europe, our health ministry is not worried about the shortage of qualified nurses in India. Britain recently stopped hiring Indian nurses for reasons that India itself is facing a shortage of qualified nurses.

CHAPTER 15

Indian Business Community A Supplement to Indentureship

The well-known merchant communities in India, Gujarathis, Sindhis, Marwadi, Chettiars (Tamil & Telugu) have now a wide presence all over the world. The word Patel is very well known in Africa and America. Ancient Indian history categorized the merchant community as Vysya. Trade between India and other countries particularly China, Arabia, Africa and the Roman Empire were carried on for many centuries. A good number of archeological and historical evidences had been unearthed establishing the fact that India had flourishing foreign trade. Roman coins were discovered, both in South and North India confirming the trade relations between India and the Romans. Indian literatures also confirm the trade relations with many countries. It is however to be noted that there is little evidence about Indian merchants settling outside India except the southeastern countries like Malaysia, Jawa and Sumatra. There might have been migration of the Indian merchant community to other parts of the world but historical evidence is not available. Religious taboo of ocean crossing could also be one of the reasons for the absence of the Indian merchant community in other trade partnering countries.

Now the Indian merchant community had carved a niche for themselves in the international business. They are now in USA, Canada, Europe, Middle East, Far East, Korea, East and South Africa. They now own from small grocer shops to multi million dollar conglomerates. Their success of course depends upon their traditional trading skill and management abilities. Apart from these business qualities, the real catalysts were their migration along with indentured labourers and the free trade policy of the European masters. Most of them started as suppliers of Indian articles to the Indian community taken as indentured labourers. The British and the Dutch also used them to procure for them a few European articles and goods from Europe. Many of them took up agencies of European made goods and contributed substantially to the marketing of western goods. They enjoyed the full protection of the colonial masters as they served the needs of both the masters and the indentured Indians. When Britain and France controlled the Red Sea with their bases in Djibouti (France) and Yemen (Britain), many Gujarathi merchants migrated from Kutch and settled in Oman, Yemen and UAE. A few Gujarathis in Oman are now Omanis with Omani passport.

The Indian merchant community which had taken shelter in Britain, France and Netherlands after banishment from African countries initially became British/French/Dutch subjects and after 10 years became British/French/Dutch citizens. Armed with the European or British passports they started moving towards USA and Europe. They operate as cartels and struggle together to eliminate rivals. Malta, a tiny island state in the Mediterranean came under British suzerainty from Italy. Indians particularly the Sindhis have flourishing businesses in textile and fancy goods when Britain turned the island into a tourist place. On the eastern side, Indians based in Hong Kong with British passports have entered the markets of Japan, Taiwan and South Korea. Although their domination is limited but their presence is very much felt by the local merchants and the competing Chinese. Southeastern Asia (Singapore, Malaysia and Indonesia) was dominated by the Tamil Chettiars and Muslims who hold the passport of these three countries.

The diamond business in Antwerp, Belgium dominated by the European Jews for over 7 centuries is now influenced by Gujarathis with British passport. More than 60% of the US$ 20 billion diamond trade is now in the hands of Gujarathis. The take over from Jews was in a phased manner without antagonising the Jewish community or the Belgian government. Patels own and manage several motels in California. The NRI merchant community has close links with India for religious and marriage purposes. As far as possible they prefer to procure raw materials for their business from India. They do not care much about nationality and are willing to do business anywhere as long as their business opportunities and religious faith are not disturbed. They also have effective contingency plans to shift their dwelling to a safer place whenever anti Indian or anti Hindu hatred erupts and drives them out of their place. India, in most cases will be the last option.

Following is another interesting quote by a frustrated European trader in South Africa.

Quote

Yet our familiarity today with this Caribbean historical phenomenon must not be seen as unique. It was part of a common assault on the Indian presence wherever he was domiciled in the British Empire. The evidence reveals that the trials and tribulations which Indian immigrants endured in countries like Mauritius, Fiji, South Africa, New Zealand, Australia, and the Caribbean were similar (2). By the turn of the nineteenth century it was not uncommon to note the unsettled nature of social relations in the various communities where Indians were becoming increasingly visible. In the West

Indies the Afro-Caribbean population felt threatened by the competition for jobs, which the presence of the Indians created. It was no less so in Fiji and Natal. By the 1890's and early 1900's the Indian presence was also threatening the commercial monopoly of the European trader in South Africa. This was vividly described in the Johannesburg Star, a British newspaper in the Transvaal in March 1899: "Apart from the question of his loathsome habits, the coolie is not an immigrant to be encouraged. He lowers the standard of comfort, and closes the avenues to prosperity to the European trader. Economically, he is of no advantage to the country he visits,—for, be it remembered that he does not settle. He accumulates money by virtue of the wretchedness in which he lives—a wretchedness constituting a terrible danger to the rest of the community—and he takes 80 per cent of that money back again to Asia. In Natal we actually have the spectacle of European trade being gradually destroyed by the impossible competition of the coolie. The Asiatic is thus a menace to the European's life, an obstacle to his commercial progress" (East Indians in Cananda's Pacific Coast 1900-14 an encounter in race relations by Sahadeo Basdeo).

Unquote

One more interesting quote about Indian merchant community particularly the Gujarathys (Little India.com The Gujarathis by Lavina Melwani)

Quote

In Migration and Cultures, Thomas Sowell observes, "Throughout East Africa, the Indian operated on a very small profit margin, lived extremely cheaply, took the risks of selling on credit, and worked long hours under what would be impossible conditions for Europeans". He quotes a British observer in the 1920s commenting that the Indians were driving their trucks, "without lights, without brakes, apparently without tires, and with an engine which looks like conking out at any moment, pushing trade through the most in accessible places".

It is this can-do attitude that the Gujarathis have carried with them to different parts of the globe. In fact, as Sowell observes, "The economic role of the Indians in Uganda can perhaps best be appreciated by considering what happened after they left. The economy collapsed".

Unquote

Non-resident Indian merchants may not be termed as coolies of the 19th century; however they cannot be elevated as independent either. The British and European masters encouraged them to service the coolies. They did not serve as coolies but definitely formed part of the indentured system. There are only one or two places where the Indian business community went and built their business independently without the protection of the British.

CHAPTER 16

Indentured Soldiers

I will be drawing the wrath of the government and armed forces if I had captioned the chapter as "Coolie Soldiers". They could have demanded the respect and honour if they had fought for India or for a cause beneficial to the International community. Most of the soldiers in British India fought for the expansion of the empire. They fought and died in the hot deserts of North Africa and cold slopes of Alps to save Britain from its enemies. I therefore personally feel that they are like any other indentured labourer or coolie. The British Indian army commanded by the East India Company had many Indian soldiers who fought against the Marathas, Sikhs, Mysoreans, Tamils, Keralites, Maharajs and Nawabs of UP, Bihar and Bengal. The British conquest of India with the able assistance of Indians was almost complete by the end of Sepoy mutiny in 1856 AD. It was surprising, rather shocking that many Maharajs in Madhya Pradesh and Zamindars in Bengal supplied men and materials to the British to crush the sepoy rebellion. The British were very successful in using the Indians against Indians through the game of divide and rule.

The game worked very well for them and they were able to gather large numbers of native soldiers. These soldiers were well utilized for conquering Afghanistan and Burma. During the first Anglo Burmese war the British Commander Archibald Campbell invaded Burma with the soldiers of the Madras regiment. The Second Burmese war was fought by General Godwin who commanded the army by name "Bengal Army" with recruits from Oudh and North Western provinces. The Anglo Afghanistan War was fought with the help of soldiers from Punjab and Uttar Pradesh. The civil rebellion that erupted in Bengal, when it was divided on religious basis by Lord Curzan in 1905 was subdued by the Gurkha regiment. The Mapla rebellion in Kerala was brutally put down by the special Madras regiment later known as the Malabar police. Thousands of Indian soldiers of Maharajas and Nawabs died during the rivalry between Britain and France to establish their colonies in India. When the British established their supremacy, all the forces of the Maharajas and Nawabs were brought under the command of the British who took them to various missions to expand their empire and influence.

During the period from 1885 to 1915, Britain organized a very strong Indian contingent commanded by English officers. The East India Company which needed protection in the initial stage from the rival European traders organised protection forces in their strong holds called Presidencies comprising both British and local troops. Obviously the leadership was always with the British. The British developed the army just to protect the interest of the company and the crown. It was not a regular army matching the prowess and technique of European army. The Indian soldiers were given the assignment of guarding the fort and important commercial places. Indian youth were excited about the new approach of the military. They liked the European style of uniforms, drill, discipline and organization. Many youngsters showed a lot of interest in joining the European army. The Governor of Pondicherry (Pudhuchery) mentioned in his diary that the Raja of Tanjore was upset and disappointed with the local youth who were more willing to join the company forces than the army of the Raja.

Robert Clive who laid the foundation of the British Empire by defeating the Nawab of Bengal in the famous battle of Plassey opened up the need to recruit more Indians to conquer their own country, which was disorganized and divided on various factors like religion, ethnicity and language. He gave the Indians the new British uniform which was later known as "Lal Pattan or the Red Coats." More units were added like cavalry and artillery; the employment of Indians in artillery was given careful attention, as it was the trump card, which brought triumph to the British in the early stages. The British policy was clear that the crucial firepower, which had the cutting edge over, the traditional Indian kings were kept out of the reach of Indian soldiers. Indians were given only the jobs of cleaning and pulling the cannons while its technical operation was exclusively handled by the British troops. Gunpowder was kept as a closely guarded secret. Native Indian troops of Maharajas and Nawabs who fought with swords and spears were no match for the firepower of the Europeans. The Nawab of Arcot who became a puppet ruler after the 3rd Carnatic War happily gifted his cavalry units to the British in exchange for their protection to his tiny kingdom near Vellore. Later cavalries from Bengal and Punjab were added to the British Indian force.

As the British became unstoppable by any Maharaja or Nawab,their army was shaping up into a regular force. New units like miners, engineers, veterinarians and physicians were added as support forces to the main army. Regular and full time army offices started functioning in all the three presidencies, Bombay, Calcutta and Madras. By 1890 AD there were a lakh of soldiers in the British Indian army and, of course most of them were Indians. The Army office equivalent to the present Ministry of Defence was created to administer the Indian soldiers who were used to conquering their own country. Fearing a concerted rebellion, the British divided the Indian forces on ethnic, religious, linguistic lines. Regiments in the name of Sikh, Rajaputana, Gurkha, Jat, Madras, Bengal, and Bombay were created with majority of the force from the respective ethnic group. This practice continues in the Indian army even now. When I questioned the rationale behind its continuance, a Major General (Retired) clarified that the intention is to give a unified feeling among the soldiers. The commanders of these regiments are generally from other states. Does it indicate that Indian army is still lacking the unified spirit? May be! The tragic comedy is that recently a central minister expressed his wish in a television interview to further divide the army by creating a new regiment for the backward community under the name Dr. Ambedkar Regiment!!

Commander Hugh Wheeler, Colonel Neil, General Havelock and Lt. Hudson, who master minded the crushing of the Sepoy Mutiny in 1856 killing thousands of Indian soldiers and innocent people were well assisted by Indian soldiers leased out from the Indian rulers of Madhya Pradesh, Rajasthan and Bengal. One of the consequences of Sepoy Mutiny was the total withdrawal of artillery from Indians. All Indian gunners were stripped of their weapons and strict vigilance was introduced to prevent the use of indigenous artillery weapons.

A well-established and organized Indian army was developed by 1860 AD to protect the interest of British in India from Indians and foreigners. The North West frontier was fortified to prevent Russian expansion into India and British rulers effectively used Indian soldiers to stop the ambitions of Russians. The British observed that the Indian soldiers never suffered from any patriotic feeling. They only grudged that their loyalty and hard work were not adequately recognized. The highest position an India soldier could achieve was that of Subedhar major and he could command only Indian soldiers. British soldiers were never put under the command of Indians. Indians were given more promotions only from 1920 due to political pressure. The Indian military academy (IMA) was established only in 1934 to train Indians for officer's position.

First World War

The First World War was a crucial test for the British, both in the home and war front. The war's immediate impact in India was its demand for manpower. The British authorities considered introducing conscription, but instead adopted a 'quota' system of procurement. Indian officials were given an ultimatum to procure a given number of men from a particular district, or face the risk of losing their jobs. The officials used bribery and even coercion to find the necessary recruits, leading to some discontent in the main recruiting grounds. The British recruited over 800,000 men from India to fight the war with Germany and Turkey. These figures included regular soldiers, medical personnel, clerks, storekeepers, cooks, lascars, messengers. Indian soldiers numbering 130,000 were placed in the western front in France to stop the Germans who were trying to enter France through Belgium. The border between France and Belgium named as the Western front was the main and crucial theatre of action in the First World War. Britain and France put up a stiff resistance, which prolonged for months. Germans complained against the use of coloured Indian troops in the European war. The Indian soldiers effectively checked german advance. The Germans used poison gas, which killed thousands of Allied soldiers including hundreds of Indians. The two decisive battles, at Nuevo Chaplle and the battle of Ypres, which restricted the German advance into France, were largely fought by Indians of the Punjab and Meerut divisions. Germany wanted to advance quickly into France before the arrival of Americans but the relentless and courageous Indians stopped them. The World War I could have changed the history of the world had the Germans not been stopped. There are many Indian names on the Menin Gate at Ypres, but the main memorial to the Indian Army on the Western Front was designed by Sir Herbert Baker, and opened in 1927 at Neuve Chaplle—the site of the Indian Corps' most famous, and costliest, action in 1915. British very sophisticatedly put in the memorial as "In Remembrance to the brave Indian soldiers who died far from home, these Indian soldiers preparing to defend and die FOR OUR freedom and liberty, fighting side by side with British soldiers." The British observed that Indian soldiers were in good spirit as they felt that fighting exhibited bravery and would bring honor. Most of them were very proud of being soldiers. They were ready to die in honour of a flag and the unit they belonged to irrespective of whether it was British or Indian. British found that different Hindi or Urdu words Izzat (Pride), Namak (loyalty expressed of taking salt) and Dharma (right deeds) were entrenched in the minds of illiterate Indian soldiers and they were ready to sacrify their life to prove the meaning of the words. A Sikh soldier, Indar Singh, fighting on the Somme in September 1916, wrote home: 'It is quite impossible that I should return alive. [But] don't be grieved at my death, because I shall die arms in hand, wearing the warrior's clothes. This is the most happy death that anyone can die'. One Indian soldier, doubting that he would survive, consoled himself with the thought that his name would be 'written in letters of gold and inscribed in the list of the brave'. British took advantage of such sentiments. They distributed the photo of King George V as a New Year card to all Indian soldiers. Indian soldiers were so excited that the King had cared for them and sent the New Year greetings. Many of them kept the King's photo in their pockets. Many men felt as though it was their duty to bring honour to their clan or caste, by fighting bravely on the battlefield. Some communities liked to imagine themselves as warriors. One of the reasons for the loyalty was purely economics. The pay for the Indian soldier was Rs. 11.00 per month, which was big money in those days for the poor and illiterate soldiers who had no means of earning back home in India. The wounded Indian soldiers were taken to military hospital in Brighton where they were treated very well but many lamented that they were kept as prisoners with all facilities. Their movements were restricted and their mails were censored, few of them compared themselves with the convicts sent to Andaman. The official estimate of the dead Indians was 64,494 but this figure appears to be only 60% of the total number of dead. The names of all of India's known war victims were carved on the main memorial to the Indian Army, the massive arch of India Gate in New Delhi. The Indians were also commemorated on the Western Front itself.

Indian troops in large numbers were withdrawn from Europe and despatched to Mesopotamia (Now Iraq). The reasons were that they could not stand the prolonged winter, which was never experienced by them in India, and the major reason was to use them against the Turkish menace. Turks, allies of enemy Germany, were threatening the British and French interests in the Middle East, particularly the British oil fields and refineries in Mosul in Iraq. The protective British Indian troops stationed in Bahrain were reinforced with a fresh contingent of newly recruited soldiers from India. The British commander Charles Townsend captured Basra and moved towards Baghdad. The Turkish forces routed him and he surrendered with 9000 troops largely Indians. British General Fenton Aylmer tried to rescue the situation but lost 21000 troops mostly Indians. This was termed as the Mesopotamia Muddle. The British in order to save and protect their interest in Iraq launched a conscription drive. The Congress party fighting for independence condemned the mobilization program. More than 300,000 Indian soldiers were recruited in 1917 and sent to Iraq. The British were able to drive the Turks from Mesopotamia and retrieve their interest at the cost of 80,000 Indian troops.

The British defence head quarters paid a great tribute to the sterling performance of Indian soldiers.

Second World War

The Second World War was another exploitation of the Indian soldiers by the British. An estimate of 2.5 million (25 lakhs) of Indian service men and women participated in the war to save the British from Germans, Italians and Japanese. Indian soldiers did the fighting in three continents, Europe, Asia and Africa. During this war Indians served in the navy and air force also. The Royal Indian navy had more than 30,000 Indians in addition to the thousands who served in the Merchant navy. Royal Indian Air Force had 50,000 Indian staff. Best performers in the air force were shifted to England to serve in Royal Air Force (RAF). Thousands of Indian women also participated in the war as nurses and as other service providers.

They fought the Italians in Eriteria, the Germans in the West African desert and the Japanese in Burma and Malaysia. Indians' contribution was significant in stopping Field Marshall Rommel who swept through the British and French army in the African desert. The battle of El Alemien was very crucial for the Allied forces; Winston Churchill remarked that the victory in the battle was the turning point of the World War 11. The 8th army under Field Marshall Montgomery that won the battle had three strong Indian divisions. The Germans were surprised by the tenacity and commitment of the Indians who stuck to their guns and continued fighting even after being cut off from their army command. It was the Indian Army units, who in the words of 'Bill' Slim (British General stationed in Middle East) were the 'best in the world' that merited recognition as superb fighting machines. Identical statements were issued by Bernard Montgomery (Monty) (Montgomery was the legendary British General) in the West. Fielα Marshal Rommel, (Rommel, an adventurous Field Marshall of the German army who commanded the Africa Corps against the

Indian Soliders in Europe First World War
Courtesy : Bharath Rakshak.com

allied forces in the African desert) the 'Desert Fox', had the 'healthiest regard' for the Indians. The Number of Indians who died in the North Africa campaign was approximately 22,000.

In the eastern front Indian involvement was substantial. The Allied army of one million troops which fought the Japanese in South East Asia included 700,000 Indian soldiers. More than 40,000 Indian troops were in the British army, which surrendered to the Japanese in Singapore. Many of them were enlisted in the Indian National Army organized by Nathaji Bose and sent to Burma for invading British India. General Bill Slim who commanded the Allied forces was able to drive the Japanese from Burma with the help of the Indian soldiers. In this war theatre Indians fought against Indians to assist the invading British and the defending Japanese.

Nethaji Subhash Chandra Bose tried to mobilize an Indian army with the help of Germans. About 3000 Indian prisoners taken by the Nazis were willing to join the army of Nethaji to fight the British but eventually used by the Germans to protect themselves from the Allied force. British, angered by the change of loyalty of the Indian prisoners unleashed derogatory information against them of having indulged in rape and killing of children while retreating with Germans from the western front.

The casualty of the Indians was estimated to be 80,000. More than 150,000 were wounded and 150,000 were taken as prisoners. The Indian Army by the end of the War was thus rated as among the best in the world whose officers and men displayed the highest levels of motivation and gallantry on the battle fields. This was the unanimous opinion of top line British generals.

Many top ranking generals from both sides (Allies and Axis) have paid great tribute to the Indian army. Dharm Pal, author of the book "Tradition of the Army" (Forward by General Carriapa and published by National Book Trust) details the gallantry of Indian soldiers in various battles. A second reading of the book will reveal that most of the heroism demonstrated by them was in favour of British East India Company during their conquest of India and their fights in the First and Second World Wars. There are no adequate or authentic record and documentation about the heroism of Indian soldiers fighting for their own kings in the past. The book mentions that Winston Churchill, the Prime Minister of Britain known for his contempt for India did not hesitate to praise the gallantry of gunners of the Madras Regiment who knocked out in one day 50 German tanks in North Africa.

The Indian army, which was hailed as the best fighting machine in the two World Wars went down in their spirit and fighting ability and cut a sorry figure during the border encounter with Chinese in 1962. Who should be blamed for this disgrace? certainly not the army but the policy makers in Delhi.

Indian soldiers, the pride of India in its war with Pakistan and China started losing the incentives and due recognition to foster their national spirit. They were also looking for opportunities to improve their livelihood after retirement. Conventions and rules were very strong that no person from the armed force can take up jobs in any military outfit outside

Nazi Swastika

Humbling of a symbol of unbridled power—Indian troops examine a captured Nazi Swastika, at Sidi Omer.

Indian Solider in West Africa Second World War
(Courtesy bharatrakshak.com)

India. Lack of war or military engagements had reduced their pride and importance. Premature retirements are becoming common in the armed forces, as the job is not very challenging to the youngsters. About 15000 officers' vacancies were not filled up during 2004/05. Armed forces advertise in the newspapers and TV inviting youngsters to join the army. When they retire they find a job of security management, which is low paying and boring. The military would have had no significance in this soft peace loving country but for the hostility shown by Pakistan since independence. Earlier corruption in the military initially was confined to the ministerial level but recently several reports appear in the media that it had percolated down to regimental level.

USA researched and found that there are thousands of retired army personnel in India who may be utilized for their campaign in Iraq. USA has a dire need for manpower, trained in military affairs as its coalition partners in Iraq campaign are now withdrawing their troops. Indians have already served in Iraq under the British during and after World War I. USA is making similar attempt on Indians. It is not as easy as before.

Reported by Siddharth Srivatsava in Asia Times (abridged).

Quote

India turned down the US request to send a peacekeeping force to Iraq. USA resorted to the back door method. Kuwaiti companies enjoying American contracts were recruiting Indians as labourers who were subsequently sent to Iraq as trained soldiers to serve the interest of American army in Iraq. Retired Indian soldiers were hired as engineers and constructions workers in various centers in Kerala, Rajastan, Punjab and Haryana. Reports revealed that ex servicemen who had combat experience and served in Indian artillery, infantry were given special attention. Srivatsava mentioned that this contingent was termed as the first ever" Indian regiment" to

THE MEMORIAL GATES
ON CONSTITUTION HILL

When you go home, tell them of us, and say: For your tomorrow we gave our today. Kohima War Memorial On 6 November 2002 HM The Queen officially inaugurated the Memorial Gates on Constitution Hill in London, UK. These Gates have been erected as a lasting memorial to honour the five million men and women from the Indian subcontinent, Africa and the Caribbean who volunteered to serve with the Armed Forces during the First and Second World Wars. They also celebrate the contribution that these men and women and their descendants, members of the Commonwealth family, continue to make to the rich diversity of British society.

work as mercenary force for the US. The assignments are generally to guard key installations like oil wells, refineries, airfields, ports and army offices, which are targeted by the militant groups. The Government of India was totally unaware of this development.

The compensation was fixed in US dollars, which became irresistible for the Indian ex servicemen. The monthly package is as follows:

A sepoy:	US$ 750 = Rs. 33500
Captain:	US$ 1250 = Rs. 56250
Major/Lt. Colonal:	US$ 1750 = Rs. 78500
Colonal:	US$ 2500 = Rs. 112500
Brigadier:	US$ 3500 = Rs. 157500

The average salary level is at least 10 times more than the pension they receive in India. The maximum age limit was fixed at 55 and should be medically fit. Soldiers who had prior experience in counter insurgency operations and fighting guerrilla attacks were given high preference. A retired colonel who returned to India after being injured said that "it is good money, but it is not hunky-dory". There seems to be no illegal trafficking in this recruitment. According to the reporter, security agencies in Mumbai and New Delhi are acting as contractors for procuring the right persons for the job by providing information to the US army authorities. Insurance cover is provided by the US army for the indentured soldiers. When this news broke out, there was lot of hue and cry by the politicians but no governmental action banning the recruitment was taken despite the possibility of leakage of sensitive defence information by the indentured service men.

Patriotic army men are reluctant to join the drive. Sepoy welfare boards in northern India appear to be siding with the unofficial deployment of Indian soldiers given the poor state of affair, of the retired servicemen.

Few service men feel that adventure in Iraq is worth taking despite the high risk as it might give a chance to exhibit their skills and talents with an attractive salary package.

Unquote

Mahatma Gandhi in 1920 initiated the non co-operation movement against the British rule. He and the Congress leaders drafted the program of mass boycott and one of the programs in the agenda was to advise the young men not to offer themselves as recruits for military service in Mesopotamia, which is now known as Iraq. Congress leaders who fought for the freedom described the British adventure with thousands of Indian soldiers as "Mesopotamian Muddle" and strongly protested the deployment of Indian soldiers to protect the British oil fields and refineries. (One of the reasons for the boycott call was to please the bullying Muslim League which showed willingness to participate in the Non-Cooperation movement after the First World War.) Retired Indian servicemen are now volunteering to go as indentured soldiers to Mesopotamia (Iraq) for the same purpose and the free Indian government does not seem much worried about it.

NRI Soldiers

The Indian government and its leaders particularly Jawaharlal Nehru right from the day of independence on Aug/15/47 gave the impression to themselves and to the world that they will stand for peace in the world. India had participated in the maximum number of UN led military operations to restore peace in conflict areas across the world. India always stood ready to send its troops for any peace keeping operation. Indian troops and commanders were involved as military observers and force commanders of UN peace keeping forces. India's reputation is very high among the Asian and African countries as they are admired for their unbiased and service oriented operation. It is no doubt a laudable gesture for world peace but our parliamentarians are least worried about the falling standards within the army. Reports appear in news papers that hundreds of young officers opt for premature retirement as they foresee that life after retirement will be financially very stressful. Our defense ministry does not have effective machinery in place to keep track of all retired persons. It is not easy either. Retired and young prematurely retired army officials and soldiers can be easily picked up by western powers that need them to fight and defend their interest in various parts of the world. In the worst scenario few may be even enlisted by terrorist gangs who are also looking for trained soldiers. UN peace keeping missions are a good contact point for identifying and hiring the available Indian soldiers. Involvement of Indian soldiers in the recent occupation of Iraq opened the gate for the hiring of Indian soldiers. The future of these disinterested ex army personnel will become like the Indian techies who wonder in foreign countries looking for jobs. Secret agencies will erupt providing opportunities for the ex soldiers. They may also become a point of contact for the enemies of the country.

There should not be NRI soldiers (!) except for UN or other recognised International operations. NRI soldiers can operate only through illegal ways as the Indian laws are very strict about hiring soldiers. The question is how far the government control is effective in restricting the outflow of Indian ex service men. There is every possibility that Indian soldiers hired through the back door method are defending the US interest in Afghanistan and they could be in the unofficial payroll of NATO forces operating under the pretext of general workers. US operations in Iraq and Afghanistan could be the pilot programs for the opening up of a new leaf in the history of Indian serfdom called NRI soldiers(!).

CHAPTER 17

Period of National Pride (1947 to 1975) Struggle to Face the Desi Reality

India won its independence without any outside help. It was a great achievement, which has no parallel in the history of any country in the world. The entire nation was very proud of their fight against the British and felt immensely pleased with their performance. The British left on a friendly note. The national spirit was running very high for few years immediately after the independence. The elders who fought for freedom and framed the structure for independent India did every thing to inject in the minds of youngsters the pride of nationalism. Apart from the official national anthem, patriotic songs in every language were sung in all schools and colleges. Unified India was growing stronger year by year. Elders were very proud of their achievement and were able to pass on the national spirit to the second generation.

The big task of running a large country with many economic/political/social handicaps was slowly realized. The cabinet, parliament and state governments started feeling the hard pinch of managing the country. The next task after independence was to make the country prosperous. India launched on the five year plans to develop the nation. The administrators struggled to meet both ends meet. The first five-year plan was a grand success, which fueled the national pride in the minds of the leaders. The dream was spread that India can become an industrial country capable of producing all the needs. The second five-year plan, despite setbacks from the Suez Canal crisis, went off well. India was able to achieve many of its targets in agriculture, industry, employment and trade. The rulers started on a massive scale of industrialization with the prime aim of providing employment. Education was made cheap and available everywhere. The number of graduates began multiplying year by year. Employment opportunities for the educated youth were limited and the politicians were cashing on the critical situation.

The government was following the socialistic pattern. Labour unions became very strong. Management of the public service units like, steel companies, were all occupied by lethargic labourers and managed by disinterested bureaucrats. Soaring unemployment was becoming a nightmare to the ruling governments. Productivity was dwindling and the need for foreign exchange to pay import bills was mounting. Imports hardly aided the exports of the country. Management in all the PSUs became helpless to arrest the falling profit and efficiency. One of the senior officers who accepted the post of the chairman of a PSU in 1965 came up with a report that retrenchment was the only way to save the company, he was removed immediately. The Government expected all the CEOs of PSUs to improve the condition magically without cutting labour cost.

The private sector was a pathetic scene. Stringent rules and regulations drove them mad. There was absolutely no incentive to improve exports. A petty clerk in the commerce, industries or finance ministry could brush aside multi crore proposals brought in by MBAs after hard work. Corruption right from the chaprasy sitting at the doorstep of the ministry to the minister was rampant. The central government was hesitant to take any bold steps to bring in reformations because of the strong opposition from the left wing, which helps the center's survival and stability. Economic aids from sympathetic western countries and Japan could not arrest the erosion of national wealth. The foreign exchange position was worsening. Stringent regulations were imposed for Foreign exchange release. It was bad that India could not afford to send a full contingent of it sports persons and players to compete in international events due to constraints of foreign exchange. Many promising players were told to arrange their own passage and lodging facilities if they want to visit and compete in events held outside India.

India's image in the international scene was worsening. Our exports were declining. External debts were mounting. Repayments of external loan became a nightmare. More debts were incurred to repay the existing debts. Our poor financial position wiped out all our glory as a nation, which can voice and represent the independent third world. Indian rupee was devalued in 1966 in order to boost exports. The impact of devaluation was more negative than positive. The real value of the Indian rupee fell drastically against hard currencies. We degenerated into a beggar nation. We continued to import food despite the sincere and serious efforts made during the five year plans. Big powers, USA and USSR hardened their stand against the begging nation. Friendly and benevolent nations who had been extending aids and soft credits tightened their generous purses. Our beggarly position became open in the international scene. Earlier, India was a guide to the African and Asian countries who achieved independence from colonial rule. They looked upon us as an example for development and growth. Later the two faces of India, one as an anti imperialist and the other as supplicant earned more pity than admiration from those Asian and African countries which till now regarded India as a role model. Humiliation at the hands of invading Chinese in 1962 added more salt to the injury.

At this juncture, the Prime Minister Indira Gandhi decided to follow what the Britishers did, encourage indentured labour. The oil boom in late seventies brought in wealth to the Gulf countries and many of them launched infrastructural developments. Arabs who were backward and illiterate could not cope with the massive development programs without help from outside. Western companies who always look for lucrative markets immediately gathered in Arabian Gulf and snatched large contracts. Their attention turned to India for the labour force required for constructional and administrative projects. Pakistan was ready to send as many labourers as possible to earn foreign exchange and also to solve its own unemployment problem. In spite of the common religious bond with Pakistan Arabs preferred Indians who had gained the reputation as trouble free and co-operative workers. The educational development during the 1960s brought out several skilled workers in India. Indira Gandhi and India had no choice but to swallow the national pride and volunteer to send the indentured labourers under government approval. Central and state ministers visited the Gulf countries at frequent intervals and showed their readiness to send as many workers as possible. This was a legalized indenture system by the free government. Kerala state government set up a special panel to exploit the opportunities in Gulf for its workers.

Free India found that the best asset of this country is the human capital. This was realized by the ruling British more than a century ago and well utilised for their colonial wealth. The exploitation was a major issue against the colonial masters as revealed by the extract from the book (The History of the Congress published in 1935) of Sri Pattabhi Sitaramayya, a veteran Congressman and a close associate of Mahatma Gandhi. This will indicate how the freedom fighters felt about the misery and shame of indentured Indian labour.

Quote

Before we proceed to narrate the events of 1920 in the sphere of Indian politics, we must refer to the celebration on the January 1st, 1920 of the abolition of the system of Indentured Labour in the colonies, which had been prevalent for well-nigh a century and by which India was directly affected. In Natal (South Africa), the Indentured Labour system was brought to an end by the refusal of the Indian Government to allow any more recruiting. In Mauritius, Indentured Labour ceased in 1911 because no more labour was required. But in other colonies in different parts of the world, the Indentured system was still being carried on. During 1914 and 1915, the Government of India made an enquiry from the governments of those provinces from which Indentured labour was taken, and it was found that the villagers were already up in arms against the Indentured system which was open to the gravest abuses. In 1915, Mr. C.F. Andrews and Mr. W.W. Pearson went out to Fiji and brought back information of the moist damaging character, which was issued, in the form of a report. This enabled Lord Harding (Viceroy of India) to accept Pundit Madan Mohan Malaviya's motion in the Imperial Legislative Council for the abolition of Indenture. But he added the ominous words that some delay must be allowed while adjustments were being made. Later in the year, it was found out that he had privately agreed with the Colonial office that recruiting should go on in India for another five years. Since it was clearly proved that such recruitment led to grave moral evils and even suicides, the government of India was challenged by Mr. Andrews whether such a private understanding did or did not exist. And when it was made public that such an understanding had been signed between the two Offices at Whitehall, Indian and Colonial, a wave of moral indignation swept the country. And Gandhi himself took up the challenge and started the anti indenture campaign in the North and the West of India. Mrs. Besant carried on the campaign in Madras. This campaign was at its height in the months of March and April, 1917 and possibly Mrs. Besant's activity in this behalf was one of the governing reasons of her internment which took place on the 15th June, 1917. Lord Chelmsford called Gandhi and realized the seriousness of the situation. A deputation of Indian ladies from every province went also to Lord Chelmsford on behalf of their Indian sisters. A date was fixed on 31st May, 1917 by Gandhi, within which the system had to be brought to an end; otherwise a Satyagraha campaign would be started in order to prevent further recruitment. On 12 April, 1917, Lord Chelmsford announced that all recruitment would be stopped as a special war-measure under the Defense of India Act. It was clear, however, that at the end of the war the whole question would be revived by the Colonies concerned, because vast financial interests were involved. Therefore Mr. Andrews on the advice of Gandhi and with the cordial consent of the poet Rabindranath Tagore, went out to Fiji again, in order to collect further facts which could be used when the question might be resuscitated at the end of the war. He spent nearly a year in Fiji and gathered far more damaging facts than on his previous visit. He also greatly interested the women of Australia in the moral question involved, and gained strong support for the abolition of the Indenture System. In March 1918, he met, Mr. Montagu at Delhi and was able to put before him the facts he had in his possession and to convince him that the system was altogether immoral. In 1919, the Government of India was able to announce that no further Indenture would be allowed and that all Indentured labourers whose five years' terms had not expired should be set free. Therefore on 1 January, 1920, there was universal rejoicing among Indians in Fiji, British Guinea, Trinidad, Surinam and Jamaica, where Indenture was still lingering, because on that day of emancipation every Indian labourer who had come out under Indenture was set free. It may be noted that this whole system was started as early as 1835 in order to supply labour to the old sugar plantations in the Colonies, which the African slaves had worked until slavery itself was abolished in 1833. It was thus a device to carry on the sugar plantations in a manner not far removed from slavery itself. Sir W. Wilson Hunter, the historian, called it "semi servile labour" and that description is accurate.

Unquote

The Act of 1921, which forced the British Government of India to stop sending indentured labours, was conveniently ignored by the governments of free India. The souls of Gopalakrishna Gokhale, Mahatma Gandhi, Annie Besant and other leaders who fought for stopping the hiring of indentured labours to Africa and Caribbean must be in a sorrowful state after the re opening of indentured labours with government blessings.

Bhograju Pattabhi Sitaramayya

Lord Stanley (who initiated the act XXXII of 1844 for Indian Indenture Labour). Courtesty : National Library of Australia

CHAPTER 18

Legalised Indenture—Start of Gulf Coolies

The Central government openly encouraged the hiring of indentured labourers. Passport offices were working in full swing.. Crowding in passport office was on the rise. Tough rules and regulations for issue of passports were withdrawn. Passport issuing offices increased their numbers to cater to need of the fast growing passport seeking workers. Several agencies sprouted for sending the workers to Gulf countries. Many hiring agencies gave false information and invoked the dream of a luxurious life and the savings potential 10 times that of India. The exodus of skilled workers started by middle of 1970s and is continuing even now.

The fitting example of a typical Gulf coolie is I (The author). Citibank, Muscat, in Sultanate of Oman hired me from Citibank Madras where I was working. The triangle formation is US employer, Indian employee and Oman the place of work. The Sultanate of Oman and other Gulf countries were very backward in 1975. Sultan Qaboos of Oman, Sheikhs of UAE, Qatar, Kuwait and Bahrain and King of Saudi Arabia decided to modernize their countries. Massive constructional programs were launched all over the Gulf. Hundreds of Indian workers were hired by multinational construction companies. Several buildings and housing projects started attracting men from India and materials from different parts of the world. They needed skilled masons, carpenters, fabricators, helpers, and general building workers, painters. As the economy depended upon importation of almost all materials from outside shipping, transport and commerce workers were in great demand. Indians readily fitted into these jobs as shipping clerks, bank clerks, insurance clerks, cashiers, drivers, electricians, launderers, cooks, janitors, security guards, typists, telex operators, office assistants, accountants and bill collectors. Knowledge of English was a great advantage for Indians to find jobs easily in the late seventies. Many banks particularly British, American and European started opening up through out Gulf and most of them are filled up by Indians. Pakistanis who wanted to have a share of the cake played the religious fiddle. Eventually the Indians had an edge over others due to their slavish attitude and superior knowledge. One Omani told me that "Indians are good but their products are bad so we prefer Indian workers and not the goods from India". The best commodity India could offer is the cheap and co-operative workers.

Advertisements for various posts started appearing in almost all newspapers. Mumbai, where the visa issuing consulates are located became crowded. Temporary chauls providing accommodation for Gulf job seekers and for waiters for visas in Mumbai did brisk business. Workers mostly from Kerala, Tamilnadu, Andhra, and Punjab crowded the Mumbai city. Streets of Colaba where the consulates are located received unusual crowd. Many treated the sidewalks of Colaba as their temporary home. Recruiting agents were working 24 hours a day and made a lot of money from providing temporary accommodation to getting air ticket. Fake educational certificates were freely available in the streets of Colaba. Mumbai received a different type of floating population. Long queues were formed in front of consulates right from 4"o clock in the morning. Health clinics sprang up and they were run by recruiting agents and doctors with no qualification were providing health certificates for the emigrants. It was not uncommon when clinics were certifying nearly 200 workers a day with all the medical tests. Airline offices and travel agents were working 16 hours a day. The service industry in Bombay was exploding. The upper class people who considered that air travel is luxurious and costly were bewildered to see masons, drivers and carpenters sitting by their side in every flight.

Arab countries were in fact emerging from the 18th century administration to the modern times. The population was small and 90% were illiterate. The oil money instead of flowing into the American and British banks was channelised towards developing their own infrastructure and living conditions. Starting from 1970 to 1995 governments found it very difficult to manage their administration and struggled very hard to co-op with the fast developments they launched. Immigration rules were very tough due to the ignorance of the locals. It is believed that the father of Sultan Qaboos, Timur himself signed all the no objection certificates issued to foreigners. Many Indians and Pakistanis, by crossing the Arabian Sea through boats, entered illegally without any passport in port cities like Muscat, Dubai, Doha and Kuwait. In Saudi Arabia, Indians went as pilgrims to Mecca and vanished in the crowd. They stayed with their friends and/or relatives until they found a job. Hundreds of Indians went as businessmen taking 72-hour visa and disappeared leaving the passport in the airport. It is reported that in 1978 there were more than 1000 Indian unclaimed passports in the Dubai airport. Thousands of Indians remained as illegal immigrants for more than 5 years. They were able to get jobs and their employers also accommodated them as they were in need of skilled labourers. Many locals found a lucrative business in Visa selling. They would establish a company, which always ended as "trading and contracting establishment". Workers permit would be obtained from the government. Their agents in Mumbai will advertise in the papers and collect the fees, which would range from Rs. 10,000 to 50,000 depending upon the place and nature of work. Recruited Indian workers would be dispatched by air. They would be received at the destination and their work permit formalities would be completed in three months time. Generally these companies will have no work. After three months the workers would be asked to find a job, which they easily got during the 70s and 80s. The work permit then was transferred to the new employer after getting a good amount from each worker. If this modus operandi misfired, the workers became steeped in debt and eventually had to come back without job. In Saudi Arabia a contractor who recruited 2000 Indian workers for two years term lost his bid for the second term of work. He arranged with the successful new bidder in such a way that he can release his men who are already experienced. He would get a sizable amount from the new bidder who could thus avoid all the formalities of recruitment. He also charged each Indian worker Saudi Riyal 500 to give release. Indian workers not only borrowed money to reach the Gulf coast but also borrowed again to get release for the new assignment. The new employer would take advantage of the helpless situation of the Indians and deprive them of many benefits like medical assistance, leave fare, proper accommodation and so on. Indians have no choice but to accept the less favorable working and living conditions. Gulf life is so infatuating that it makes many Indians stick around even if the life style and job status deteriorate. The demand for Indian labor was so much that sometimes-even doctors and professionally qualified engineers and accountants were brought in under visas such as drivers, pharmacists and mechanics. This was due to the local regulations, which forbid import of qualified professionals from India in order to give opportunities for Arabs and Pakistanis. I know a well-known British Chemical company brought in its finance mangers who were qualified Chartered Accountants from India under driver's visa. Arab entrepreneurs were ruthless in treating the Indians. Many contracting companies did not pay regular salaries and the promised benefits. The labour courts in Gulf were very primitive as there were no labour laws. The pitiable situation was that the labourers got little help from the Indian embassy whenever they were in trouble.

The living conditions of these immigrant Indians were pathetic. Accommodation was a big problem between 1975 and 1985. Many labourers lived on the terrace of buildings. Regular workers who were not fortunate enough to be employed by a decent employer lived in small rooms. These were like the three tier railway compartments with 10 workers in a small room of 12′ x 12′. There will be a common kitchen manned by the workers themselves. Their only pastime was viewing Indian movies in the video recorder. Bazaars were always crowded with Indians in groups chatting and discussing on the Friday evenings. One of the common topics was the Indian rupee rate of exchange. Discussion on sending money through havala was also discussed among low paid laborers. Post offices used to be crowded during Thursdays with Indians buying stamps for their letters. The postal system was inefficient due to lack of manpower. Indians who are lucky to be employed by well established European or American companies lead a luxurious life with tax-free income. Electronic gadgets like tape recorder, video recorder, camera and gold biscuits, perfumes/cosmetics and foreign liquors were the main purchases of the Indians when these articles were rare in India at that time. Incoming Gulf flights would be loaded with big suitcases full of these items and the customs officials in ports of entry made a good fortune by exploiting the ignorant labourers.

The Indian embassy's role in solving the miserable conditions of labour was totally ineffective, as they never got the respect from the local government officials. Hundreds of cases of non-payment of salaries and benefits, ill treatment, sexual harassments of Indian ayahs were reported to the Indian embassy but their efforts to solve the plight of the Indians were ineffective. As the complaints were mounting month by month, the best Indian embassy could do was to file the complaints in a folder and keep a record. The Indian embassy used to work 16 hours a day for the renewal of passports and change of profession in the passports. It was extremely difficult to get an appointment from the Ambassador or the First Secretary. Few ambassadors did take real efforts to streamline the process of passports and also developed rapport with local officials to solve the labour problems.

The Indians who went to the Gulf countries may be called the pioneers of NRIs. NRI (Non Resident Indian) is the sophisticated legal title given to an indentured modern Indian coolie. Their main complaint with the government of India is that their welfare in the host country is not at all well looked after by the embassy of India. Their main problems are the dishonour of the contract terms by the employers in terms of salary and benefits, cumbersome and expensive (around US $ 800) procedure in the event of death of labour either by accident or suicide. There is absolutely no program or procedure in any embassy to meet the Indians and find out their problems. Unlike the US embassy, where the US citizen has the right for an appointment with the ambassador, Indian NRIs particularly in Gulf, have difficulties in voicing their grievances to the ambassador. The Indian government also seems to be following the policy of non interference with local problems fearing that other SAARC nationals could replace Indians. This might result in the reduction, if not total loss of nearly $ 4.0 billion remittance from the Gulf region every year.

Gulf NRIs blame that the ministry established for NRI affairs cares only for the NRIs in USA, Hong Kong, and Europe because most of the Indians in these countries are wealthy and affluent unlike the crowd of monthly salary receiving Indians in Gulf. Gulf NRIs are also very upset that whenever they organize a gathering or seminar low-key officials attend it from the NRI ministry. It may be due to less importance given to the ministry itself in the cabinet. Gulf Indians are also ignorant about the limitations and inability of the Government of India on these local matters. The embassy officials are also tired of solving problems of complicated matters like getting compensation for death and accident, termination or end of contract benefits. It is not uncommon that middle level companies dodge the employees by not giving the end of contract benefits and return airfare. Indian media never fails to report with lament the atrocities of the Gulf employers or the sufferings of employees. Recently many Indians died of a fire accident in Bahrain; the incident was flashed in almost all India newspapers and magazines sympathising with the victims. The matter was forgotten within a week's time. Recruitments to Bahrain will continue, may be for the same company to replenish men who died in the accident. Annie Besant in her book "Birth of New India." deplored the indentured labour.

Quote

He (indentured labourerer) is not a property like the regular slave; he is a slave on loan for whom there is no responsibility when loan expires.

At least Indians need not be so careless of human life honour; so careful of what is truly in this case of "Filthy lucre". Let them warn the villagers in every recruiting district; let them hang around the offices of Registering Magistrate and officials; and warn the men and women not to sign the agreement to emigrate, explaining them that they are giving themselves into slavery. Let them spread the knowledge of the conditions, of murders, hanging, suicides, shameless voice, absence of all decency, the reckless despair which drives men to death. Let us agitate, agitate, and agitate until the law is changed. Let us cry aloud in all villages haunted by the recruiter that he is leading men and women into very hell.

Unquote

The Governments of free India are not serious about these incidents of human disaster nor do they have any plan to take care of the ignorant and innocent villagers falling into the trap of the agents. The Gulf craze remains strong among building workers. Labour agents are able to mislead the innocent and make a fortune. It is reported that the victims of Bahrain disaster paid as much as Rs. 15 lakhs to get the job.

Several hundreds of Indian labourers are still struggling to make a minimum decent life in Far East and Middle East. The pesent situation and procedures are different from the administration of British India. However the dream of better life abroad is still lingering the minds of many Indians.

The inefficiency of the Government of India in protecting the rights and privileges of unskilled and semi skilled Indian workers abroad is an open secret. It is time that dedicated (!!) politicians and NGOs take up this issue seriously and educate the innocent unemployed youth.

The situation since 1836 AD had not changed.

Indian population was just 10,000 in 1948; many of them were taken by the British oil and shipping companies and consulate. Indians were dominant in the British consulate as very few Britishers were willing to come to the region due to harsh weather condition. The current estimated number of Indians in Gulf and Middle East is around 3 million providing services in various capacities. The unique feature about Gulf Indians is that of a comprehensive coverage of all professions excepting lawyers and politicians, who are banned. Indians are very proud that without them developments in these countries would not have been possible. Arabs look at Indians as a timid, hard working and highly compromising work force in the world.

NRIs

There are a few NRIs in every country who enjoy high positions and prestige like Lakshmi Mittal, Salman Rushdie, Swaraj Paul, Boby Jindal, Kewalram Chenrai, Vikram Pandit, Amar Gopal Bose, Sabeer Bhatia, Kavitark Shriram, Vinodh Khosla, Ramani Iyer, Sunita Williams, Indira Nooyi and a few more wealthy business persons in Australia, Canada, Hong Kong and Malaysia. Indian government and Indian media always put these couple of dozens of people in lime light and try to project that India is a great country. A cabinet minister recently announced that 38% of doctors in USA are Indians and 36% of scientists in NASA are Indians. The minister also proudly revealed that 34% of Microsoft Corporation, 28% of IBM Corporation and 17% of Intel Corporation is Indians. It is obvious that the Ministries of External Affairs and Human Resources have absolutely no idea or clue about the thousands of low paid, toiling and tortured Indian workers all over the world. They do not care as these labourers are non entities unless grave accidents take place attracting the media. The elite Indians form less than 0.001% of the total living or surviving in foreign countries as part of the modern coolie trade. Those who had settled and became citizens or subjects of the host country could be less than 20% of the total and are termed by the Indian government as people of Indian origin (POIO).

It is found out that Indians either NRIS or POIOs are spread out in more than 100 countries and the estimated strength is around 20 million (2 crores). There are a few thousands suffering as stateless people. More than 90% of the total have gone to foreign countries in search of jobs and do low profiled jobs.

The emigration started with 216 workers from Kolkatta to the Caribbean in 1836 AD. It has reached the figure of 2 crores in a span of 170 years. This figure is likely to go up further in future as the west is trying to exploit the last frontier in the world and it is Africa. Middle and lower Africa are still backward and there are ample opportunities for exploration as well as exploitation. West have the experience of managing the Indians in this region. Another tide of Indians moving under the Union Jack or American flag can be expected in the near future.

(Appendix 4 gives detail of NRIs and PIOs all over the world)

Ministry for Overseas Indians (MOI)

MOI was established in 2004 to address the needs of NRIs and PIOs. This central ministry takes care of the Indian workers and assists NRIs with information about opportunities in India. They provide information and guidance in the areas of education, business investments, housing and a few more. The draft plan and presentations are all very impressive. How long will their plans be effective in improving the standards and security of the thousands of low paid workers. The MOI is soliciting a standard form of contract for the workers which will ensure their rights and privileges. This is not very easy as the MOI is at the receiving end. Recent reports reveal that India had agreed not to insist on the minimum wages payable for different categories of labour working in the Gulf region. It is targeting gulf countries where the manual and semi skilled labourers are struggling for the last 3 decades. There is a proposal to create a NRI fund from the union budget allocation to serve the suffering Indian workers. The fund will be utilized to take care of the Indians whose benefits were denied by their foreign employers and also help them to relocate into India with minimal financial burden. All these proposals are good in paper and its enforceability is a big question. The

Foot soldiers' bunker: Invisible workers behind the glitz of Dubai catch a little rest before returning to work. (Photo: © 2005 Steve Raymer) Courtesy : yaleglobalonline.com

administrative task is not easy and we can expect several media reports about the misuse of this fund.

MOI has a department for Diaspora services. The aim is to lure the NRIs and PIOs to invest in India or use their influence to get political and economic benefits for India. Pravasi Bharathiya Samman (PBS), part of MOI aims to induce the Indian feeling among the POIOs by awarding titles and projecting them as a celebrity. Indian media gives wide coverage for the achievements of these Indians who have become citizens of the domiciled country. Reports are coming out that a state in USA was not happy when PBS honoured a PIO. The host country will tolerate this new development to some extent and may consider this kind of special awards as unnecessary intrusion into their affairs.

MOI can only operate as moral support to the Indian workers. It has absolutely no direct diplomatic or legal control on the Indians working in foreign countries. They have to go through the local authority which may or may not co operate with Indian embassy which depends upon the relationship between the two countries.

CHAPTER 19

Indenture within India Start of Cyber Coolies

The era of cyber coolies started from 1990 and it is still continuing. According to Barbara Crutchfield George & Deborah Roach Gaut of California State University, Long Beach the initiative was taken by Jack Welch, CEO of General Electric (GE) who envisioned that India has the best working class fit for service providing industry. GE made a business partnership with Wipro to sell its medical systems and equipments. During the late 1980s software corporations in USA hired local techies to develop their programs. Individual soft ware engineers particularly IITians who worked in USA for 3 to 4 years got the sub contract from their employers to program their requirements. It was during Manmohan Singh"s tenure as finance minister the opening up of the country for free trade took place. Restrictions on foreign exchange, travel, and foreigner's investments into India were systematically reduced and finally lifted. When the western corporations entered with least restriction on their activities and business they rediscovered the vast labour potential with a distinct cost advantage. History is been repeated in a different style.

USA, Singapore and UK opened their gates for professionally qualified Indians to compile and compute programs. Initially a few Indians were imported by big MNCs like IBM, Microsoft, Dell, Intel and others. They were looking for IItians and B.Techs. The Indian techies contributed substantially to the growth of big technology firms like Sun Micro Systems, Microsoft, Oracle and many others. The name of the Indians as efficient and knowledgeable technological experts started spreading. Very soon Americans found a huge army of Indian techies available for their growth. John Reed the CEO and chairman of Citicorp during his visit to India in 1991 was astonished to see the huge potential available in India. He remarked "India, a tiger uncaged". Citicorp without wasting its time floated a huge technology company and started hiring hundreds of fresh engineering graduates at very attractive salary and perks. Indian boys and girls were very happy to do innovative computer programs for the entire operation of Citicorp worldwide. The success story of Citicorp spread like wild fire among the leading tech firms in USA and India. Indian firms like Wipro, Infosys, TCS, HCL tech immediately took steps and offered to service the needs of US and European corporations. This is very nicely termed as software export. Every week hundreds of software engineers left for various destinations in the west mostly to USA. The Y2K program, which threatened the world, attracted many Indians to work in USA to avert any disaster by the computer program, which did not take into consideration the year 2000 in its computation. Thousands of Indian engineers were hired on temporary basis to set right the Y2K deficiency in the systems. Planeloads of software engineers were imported in Britain and USA. The technology boom was accelerating all over USA. It was the technology boom that made Indian software engineers most wanted in the employment market. Many tech. firms grabbed Indians who reached USA on temporary visa. San Jose the Silicon Valley had turned into a mini India. The US government had laid down minimum wages for immigrants, which were very comfortable for Indians. The growing concentration of Indians in important technological centers like San Jose, Boston, Washington, and Austin became an eye sore for many native Americans. They found the Indians living a better life than them. The situation became so critical that George Bush in his poll campaign said that he would give America back to Americans. This hatred however did not flare up like the anti Indian campaigns of 19th century. He won the election and took immediate steps to roll back the carpet for the Indians. Thousands of Indians were sent back after the Y2K program. Thousands of Indians who constructed the B 2B (Business to Business) program lost their job. It (B2B) was ridiculed as "Back to Bombay/Bangalore". US tech firms that admired the mathematical abilities of Indians did not want to loose their knowledge. They lobbied and got all their operation transferred to India one by one. It created a huge unemployment problem in USA. More than 3 million jobs were lost in 2 years period. Technology had improved so much that the Indians could now service the US companies sitting in their own home.

Western countries have now found again coolies who are educated, and as usual very obedient and receptive. This time there is no need to give transportation or initial lodging and boarding expenses. They can be slave driven with their own masters in their own destination. This modern slavery is not practiced in a tea/coffee/sugar cane garden or on the decks of ships or in the battlefields or in a construction site in Arab countries. This is now called call centers, Business processing outsourcing centers and offshore centers. The modern slaves sit inside air-conditioned halls with all facilities for eating and entertainment. Their masters are far away yet they hold strict control on the quality of performance. The modern Mesthries (supervisor) are well established technology Desi companies. They make sure that the cyber coolies do their job to the entire satisfaction of the western masters sitting in London/New York/Frankfurt/and many more cities in United States of America. Cyber coolies are often taken out to far away destinations like USA, Europe and Far East to promote the business of the western masters. They will be engaged in solving technical problems or sit with customers and fulfill their computing requirements.

Technology companies boast that they export software to foreign countries. The income statements of big names like Wipro, Infosys, TCS, Satyam and Polaris will indicate that their main source of income is handling routine daily/monthly/quarterly/yearly transactions of customers all over the world particularly in USA. British masters in Caribbean during the last century offered two options to the garden coolies. (1) Return to India with lump sum of money or (2) Continue your work with a possibility of citizenship, which enables owning lands for self-cultivation. Cyber coolies were also offered similar option. Many of those who went on a mission from India took this option offered by their customers. It may not be citizenship with land ownership rather it could be a green card or a permanent residence status for a long period with a job stable enough to secure a decent living. These kinds of offer however were not possible in Gulf or Far eastern countries where the masters themselves were aliens. United States is the ultimate goal for many upcoming Desi techies.

A call center in India serving American clients. Many of the vanished white collar jobs in the US are reappearing in low-wage countries.
(Photo: intellicomcenters.com)
Courtesy : yaleglobalonline.com

CHAPTER 20

Start of Self Inflicted Indenture

It all started with type setting for foreign books and journals. Self inflicted indentureship began in 1993 by medical transcription which created thousands of offshore secretaries and stenographers. They were trained to do the writing for western insurance companies who maintain the health record narrated by the physicians. The staff required for this business is expected to reach around 170,000. Six years later BPOs sprouted all over south India, Bombay and New Delhi. Bangalore became the hub for cyber coolies. This time the coolies have to be educated with technical knowledge and proficiency in English language. The word recruitment has been sophisticatedly changed into placements. The Kankanis or the Girmits have changed their names to placement agencies or HRD consultants. The garden coolies were limited to gardens like tea, sugar, coffee, rubber and coco; a few were used for constructional activities like railroad building and forest clearing. The cyber coolies do almost all the back office jobs of various industries. They include, handling of insurance claims, payroll accounting, tax accounting, credit card processing, fixing computer problems through telephone, housing loans enquiries and accounting, consumer loans accounting, pension accounting and many more. The voluminous job of data entry and processing are like clearing, tilling, watering and harvesting 1000 acres of land; it is not worth keeping an expensive European or American when cheap coolies from India are available. Software programs involve 1000s of man-hours for coding, compiling and data entering. The big corporations in USA and Europe follow a policy to outsource all the clerical, routine and all kinds of necessary but low profiled jobs like customer enquiries to India and concentrate on core business like planning, R&D and managerial control. All odd jobs relating to these functions are also outsourced to India.

Masters of the 19th century preferred Indians from UP, Bengal and Bihar because they were experienced in agriculture. Cyber masters prefer Indians from the souths who according to them are good in mathematics and also obedient. A comparative study reveals that the garden coolies and cyber coolies have a lot of common features. The labor brokers sold dreams to the innocent peasants of high income and better living conditions. Peasants who were frustrated by the local social and economic conditions preferred to leave India. The hardship of the job was felt after 3 months in both cases. Placement agencies are doing the same to the young graduates showing the carrot of high salary and modern working conditions like air-conditioned office, cafeteria, entertainment area, staff loans, generous bonus, attractive titles, foreign assignments and possibilities of quick promotion and so on. This new working environment is totally alien to the average Indian type of office set up. The daily work of both coolies is the same. Garden coolies dealt with plants like plucking tea leaves, removing weeds, trimming the branches, watering and other related manual works whereas cyber coolies sit in front of the computer wearing the head set answering calls, inputting data, logging complaints and requests, following up with customers whom they never see, soliciting new products and schemes. Garden coolies were under the close supervision of the master. Absenteeism, disobedience and mistakes were punished by flogging or beaten in the public. Few were shut up in isolated dens. These were all in addition to usual cut in wages and benefits. Performance of cyber coolies are monitored on a daily basis with the aid of special feed back information system loaded in the computer. The job of Mesthries (supervisor or overseer) is done by close circuit cameras, which captures time wasted by way of chit chatting, reading magazines or playing games in the computer. Cyber coolies are under obligation to meet daily targets. Mistakes and drop in performance quality are given warning and consecutive three warnings lead to loss of job. Cyber masters will filter out unproductive and non co-operative employees. It is easy for them to get immediate replacements from the market. This was not possible with plantation work. An unproductive garden coolie had to be corrected by ways of punishments, coercion and motivation. Workers cannot be fired as the company was under obligation to send them back to India and there were no replacements readily available. A Fired cyber coolie can easily get a job under present circumstance whereas garden coolie, if fired, had to return to India where he would have to face the agony of getting a job.

Long hours of work are common to both. The garden coolie worked 10 hours a day and almost 7 days a week. Several reports are available about the ill health developed by garden coolies due to overwork and harsh working conditions. The normal working hours of call centers and BPOs are from 6.00pm to 7.00am. This odd Indian time matches the regular time of 9.00am to 5.00pm of USA where the customers are living. Heavy pressure of work and odd timing lead to physical and mental fatigue and lead to body ache, insomnia, gastro irregularities, loss of weight and mental depression. Irregular eating habits lead to excess smoking and drinking. Health further deteriorates when they suppress all the symptoms of weakness in order to keep the job or to score higher ratings for promotion. All indentured labourers swallowed their grievances and insults and tried hard to settle down as they normally paid a lot of money to the labour agents, which had to recover. Similarly the cyber coolies whose parents had spent a lot of money for their education try to adjust themselves bearing all the disappointments until such time they could recoup the education expenses. Garden masters were lenient with religious celebrations of the coolies and allowed them to take a day off. Cyber coolies who toil 24 hours for the western masters are not given holidays for Diwali, Janmashtami, Eid, Independence day, Republic day, Gandhi Jayanthi, Gurunanak's birthday if these occasions do not fall on a Saturday or Sunday whereas they are let off for Independence Day of USA (4 July), Martin Luther's day, Thanks giving day and so on. The names of the Indian slaves who were traded by the Europeans in the Cape of Good Hope were changed into Christian names. It is reported that few call centers in Chennai and Bangalore give western names to their employees like Peter, Sam, Clara as the customers of US and European masters find it difficult to pronounce the Indian names.

There were no unions in the gardens. However there were several mass representations made to voice their grievance. The British governors took pity on them and enacted laws to protect their basic rights and privileges. Cyber world is so far not unionized. The exploited coolies are brainwashed that they are part of the management as they receive higher salaries and benefits. The left leaders who are keenly watching the development in this industry will one day force formation of labour unions in call centers and BPOs; it is only a matter a of couple of years. Managers will be surprised to see an overwhelming support for unions from the coolies, as the exploitation is frightening and devastating. The cry that the knowledge and talents of educated youth are being wasted by sitting with a headphone and answering the impatient and often rude enquiries of the far away customers is getting louder.

CHAPTER 21

Establishment of Offshore East India Companies

A New York management consultant remarked that the wings of the Angel is designed in heaven but made in hell where the labour is cheap. US and European MNCs started shifting their back office operation to India since 1990. MNCs in the fields of engineering, pharmaceuticals, chemicals and design have opened their research centers in India. Thousands of highly qualified engineers are hired at very lucrative salary package to carry out research projects for them. University students are also encouraged to involve in this business. Reputed educational institutions send their students to undertake project works for MNCs during their vacation. The research does not originate in India, the basic requirement is conveyed by the masters and the Indian centers are asked to collect data, compile programs, make testing and provide solutions. These tedious tasks are done by the Indians to facilitate the western scientists. Trials before implementation will also be carried out in India. The end products will be introduced in USA or Europe where they will be patented and sold back to India at a high price. This is similar to the production of tea in India and Sri Lanka but the international price for tea is fixed and traded in

London commodity exchange, which governs the local tea price. General Electric of USA established a huge research center called JFWTC in the name of GE' s chairman Jack Welch near Bangalore and has an army of Indian PhDs working for their research requirements. Big names like IBM,Cisco System, Du Pont have started moving their R&D to India. Reports indicate that JFWTC had filed over 400 patents from the research conducted in their Bangalore centre. Microsoft had filed over 80 patents developed from its Hyderabad research centre.

The move to transfer R&D works is only to take advantage of the lower operation cost and the receptiveness of an average Indian and not in recognition of his/her knowledge or talent.

Statistics and projections made by Nasscom(National Association of Software companies) aggravate the dreams of youngsters and education marketers. Projections of politicians and consultants are framed in such a way that there will not be any job in USA and Europe since all are being systematically transferred to India. USA transferred more than 800,000 jobs to India since 2002 and expected to move around 3,000,000 million jobs in the next 10 years. The average annual income in India is just $700, versus $42,000 in the United States. Even a college-educated Indian worker earns less than 30% of his American counterpart. He or she is also willing to work 12-hours a day and six days a week. That's why U.S. companies are expected to employ more than 3.0 million service workers in India by 2010. Almost 75% of the Fortune 500 companies had shifted significant size of their back office to India. The revenue of outsourcing in India is estimated to be US $ 14.00 billion. This revelation is true to some extent but all of them invariably omit either by ignorance or deliberately to accept that all the routine jobs and assignments in which there is significance cost advantage are only transferred. A survey made in USA revealed that 64% of the surveyed were for cost advantage. American companies are holding on to the high-skilled work that requires face-to-face interaction, while jobs that can be done "over the wire" get shipped to India. The scene is very much like what we can see in a mechanic shed where the chief mechanic will repair the machine and the apprentice boys will tighten the nuts and bolts, grease and polish the machines before handing over to the customers.

Following figures mitigate the above inference. The geographical distribution of the revenue reveals that USA and Europe are serviced more by the big fours (TCS, Infosys, Wipro and Sathyam) of India. The true information is that these two are the major IT spenders of the world and India provides the necessary services which are mainly back office operations and network maintenance.

Table of geographical distribution of revenue of the IT majors.

(Year 2005)	*Sathyam*	*TCS*	*Infosys*	*Wipro*
Total Revenue (Rs. Crore)	3546	2249	6860	5423
Geogrphical location of IT Global Rev.				
USA	64.6%	61.3%	65.2%	63%
Europe	18.9%	24.7%	22.3%	32%
Japan/Pacific	1.5%			4.0%
Rest of world	6.4%	5.1%	10.6%	
India	4.2%	8.9%	1.9%	1.0%

Letters from Indian companies similar to the letter of Gillanders & Arbuthnot would have reached several US and European corporations offering the best Indian service at the lowest possible cost.

CHAPTER 22

Diary of an East India Company Surveyor

Dozens of surveys must have been conducted on the benefits of outsourcing low profiled jobs to India. The cheap educated labour pool is a panacea to the big corporations. They can survive in the western business only if they can maintain the shareholders value; cutting cost is the popular way to achieve it.

Writer Pete Engardio (Business Week, Jan/25/06) gave the following few information in his article "Why outsourcing to India is a great idea". This sample writing by the masters of outsourcing gives an idea about how they look at and handle outsourcing to India.

Quote

Want to survive? Outsource!

More aggressive outsourcers are aiming to create radical business models that can give them an edge and change the game in their industries. Old-line multinationals see off shoring as a catalyst for a broader plan to overhaul outdated office operations and prepare for new competitive battles. And while some want to downsize, others are keen to liberate expensive analysts, engineers, and salesmen from routine tasks so they can spend more time innovating and dealing with customers.

"This isn't about labour cost," says Daniel Marovitz, technology-managing director for Deutsche Bank's global businesses. "The issue is that if you don't do it, you won't survive."

The new attitude is emerging in corporations across the US and Europe in virtually every industry. Ask executives at Penske Truck leasing why the company out sources dozens of business processes to Mexico and India, and they cite greater efficiency and customer service. Ask managers at US-Dutch professional publishing giant Wolters Kluwer why they're racing to shift software development and editorial work to India and the Philippines, and they will say it's about being able to pump out a greater variety of books, journals, and Web-based content more rapidly.

Ask Wachovia Corp., the Charlotte (N.C.)-based bank, why it just inked a $1.1 billion deal with India's Genpact to outsource finance and accounting jobs and why it handed over administration of its human-resources programs to Lincolnshire (Ill.)-based Hewitt Associates.

Smart use of off shoring can juice the performance of established players, too. Five years ago, Penske Truck Leasing, a joint venture between GE and Penske Corp., paid $768 million for trucker Rollins Truck Leasing Corp.—just in time for the recession. Customer service, spread among four U.S. call centers, was inconsistent.

"I realized our business needed a transformation," says CFO Frank Souza. He began by shifting a few dozen data-processing jobs to GE's huge Mexican and Indian call centers, now called Genpact. He then hired Genpact to help restructure most of his back office. That relationship now spans 30 processes involved in leasing 216,000 trucks and providing logistical services for customers.

Now, if a Penske truck is held up at a weigh station because it lacks a certain permit, for example, the driver calls an 800 number. Genpact staff in India obtains the document over the Web. The weigh station is notified electronically, and the truck is back on the road within 30 minutes.

Before, Penske thought it did well if it accomplished that in two hours. And when a driver finishes his job, his entire log, including records of mileage, tolls, and fuel purchases, is shipped to Mexico, punched into computers, and processed in Hyderabad.

In all, 60% of the 1,000 workers handling Penske back-office process are in India or Mexico, and Penske is still ramping up. Under a new program, when a manufacturer asks Penske to arrange for a delivery to a buyer, Indian staff helps with the scheduling, billing, and invoices. The $15 million in direct labor-cost savings are small compared with the gains in efficiency and customer service, Cocuzza says.

Big Pharma is pursuing huge boosts in efficiency as well. Eli Lilly & Co.'s labs are more productive than most, having released eight major drugs in the past five years. But for each new drug, Lilly estimates it invests a hefty $1.1 billion. That could reach $1.5 billion in four years.

"Those kinds of costs are fundamentally unsustainable," says Steven M. Paul, Lilly's science and tech executive vice-president. Outsourcing figures heavily in Lilly's strategy to lower that cost to $800 million

The drug maker now does 20% of its chemistry work in China for one-quarter the U.S. cost and helped fund a startup lab, Shanghai's Chem-Explorer Co., with 230 chemists. Lilly now is trying to slash the costs of clinical trials on human patients, which range from $50 million to $300 million per drug, and is expanding such efforts in Brazil, Russia, China, and India.

Other manufacturers and tech companies are learning to capitalize on global talent pools to rush products to market sooner at lower costs.

On Stor Inc., a Los Gatos (Calif.) developer of storage systems, says its tie-up with Bangalore engineering-services outfit HCL Technologies Ltd. enables it to get customized products to clients twice as fast as its major rivals.

"If we want to recruit a great engineer in Silicon Valley, our lead time is three months," says CEO Bob Miller. "With HCL, we can pick up the phone and get somebody in two or three days."

But IndyMac also credits its aggressive offshore outsourcing strategy, which Consumer Banking CEO Ashwin Adarkar says has helped make it "more productive, cost-efficient, and flexible than our competitors, with better customer service." IndyMac is using 250 mostly Indian staff from New York-based Cognizant Technology Solutions Corp. to help build a next-generation software platform and applications that, it expects, will boost efficiency at least 20% by 2008.

IndyMac has also begun shifting tasks, ranging from bill collection to 'welcome calls' that help US borrowers make their first mortgage payments on time, to India's Exlservice Holdings Inc. and its 5,000-strong staff.

In theory, it is becoming possible to buy, off the shelf, practically any function you need to run a company. Want to start a budget airline but don't want to invest in a huge back office? Accenture's Navitaire unit can manage reservations, plan routes, assign crew, and calculate optimal prices for each seat.

Have a cool new telecom or medical device but lack market researchers? For about $5,000, analytics outfits such as New Delhi-based Evalueserve Inc. will, within a day, assemble a team of Indian patent attorneys, engineers, and business analysts, start mining global databases, and call dozens of US experts and wholesalers to provide an independent appraisal.

Want to market quickly a new mutual fund or insurance policy? IT services providers such as India's Tata Consultancy Services Ltd. are building software platforms that furnish every business process needed and secure all regulatory approvals.

A sister company, Tata Technologies, boasts 2,000 Indian engineers and recently bought 700-employee Novi (Mich.) auto- and aerospace-engineering firm Incat International PLC. Tata Technologies can now handle everything from turning a conceptual design into detailed specs for interiors, chassis, and electrical systems to designing the tooling and factory-floor layout.

"If you map out the entire vehicle-development process, we have the capability to supply every piece of it," says Chief Operating Officer Jeffrey D. Sage, an IBM and General Motors Corp. veteran.

Unquote

Courtesy : www.rediff.com / businessweekonline.com

Above is one of the several survey reports produced for the benefit of MNCs.

CHAPTER 23

Spread of Indenture within India

The open door policy of India is well exploited by MNCs who want to try dangerous and hazardous chemicals, and drugs on Indians. Clinical trials for testing the side effects and potency of the drugs till now conducted in the country of manufacture are now being shifted to India. Thousands of poor are likely to be targeted by pharmaceutical MNCs who can conduct trails not only at cheap price but also the forbidden experiments in USA and Europe. The compensation if claimed for any mistake, which might cause loss of lives, will be meager sums easily affordable by them. Indian legal protection to victims is not as strong and powerful as in the west. Complaints or opposition from public or from NGOs may not be given any due importance. Western countries make big hue and cry for using animals like monkeys and pigs for clinical testing. Indians are more than willing to undergo these tests. In the month of July/06 the Union Health Minister said in a gathering arranged by John Hopkins School of Public health, Washington that "India is not a guinea pig for clinical trails". In August/06, just a month after, the news appeared that "India's clinical outsourcing market to grow sizably". This is nothing but clinical trials and research outsourcing. Contract Research

Organisations (CRO) are on the growth path in India, A leading Clinical Research International company an arm of US corporation made projection that market size in India is closer to US$ 1.0 billion and it might reach the level by year 2010 AD. CROs in India are luring the US and European corporations to enter India a fertile ground for their experiments. The numbers of people suffering from cancer, diabetic, asthmatic, cardiac, cataract, HIV related deseaces and other major ailments run into millions. The co operation from patients for tests is assured. Above all these advantages is the weak legal protection available to the victims. Indian government and its bureaucrats may not take it seriously until it reaches an ugly situation.

Following is the information in the web site of a CRO which is actively soliciting the clinical trails to be conducted in India. It was captioned as India Advantage.

- Huge patient base
- Diversity of diseases
- Heterogeneous population mix
- Drug naïve population
- High enrollment rates
- Good patient compliance/retention
- State-of-the-art hospital facilities
- Reliable, well-trained, experienced investigators
- Source data in English
- Demonstrated ICH GCP quality standards
- Competitive costs
- Good communication network and IT capabilities
- Increasingly accommodating regulatory environment
- 40 million asthmatic patients
- ~34 million diabetic patients
- 8-10 million people HIV positive
- 8 million epileptic patients
- 3 million cancer patients
- > 2 million cardiac related deaths
- 1.5 million patients with Alzheimer's disease

- 15% of population is hypertensive
- 1% of population suffers from schizophrenia

Hospitals	14,000
Doctors	500,000
Hospital beds	700,000 (85% urban)
Medical colleges	162
Medical graduates	17,000/year

This is similar to the letter of Gilanders & Arbuthnot who solicited Indians in 1836 AD as indentured labour for M/s. Gladstone, a plantation manager in the Caribbean? Nothing seemed to have changed since 1836 AD; indentured labour is disguised under the sophisticated word 'Globalisation". Ruthless brokers are eagerly waiting for the opening up of this business. Although sale of human organ legally prohibited in India, human organ trafficars are very active in the black market. Recently news flashed that 50 women(!) in a fishermen village near Chennai sold their kidneys for Rs. 40,000. Police later unearthed a big kidney racket. Organ agents will have a well diversified market for their operation if the CROs are given a free hand.

Hospitals in India are now wooing the Americans and Eropeans to have their medical treatment in India. This started after USA permitted medical treatment in selected Asian countries including India to take cost advantage. Treatment and operations of heart, brain, kidneys, and stone removals cost less than 40% of its American counterpart. What it might cost $ 100,000 in USA will cost only $ 12000 in India. Cataract eye operation costs Rs.180,000 in UK whereas the same inclusive of travel and accommodation will cost only Rs. 65000 in Chennai. In the olden days patients went to Europe or USA for better and advanced treatment for their illness. India does not boast about advanced treatment but attracts thorough low cost treatment. The message is very clear that cheap medical labour (doctors and surgeons) is also available in India. This is given a new name "Medical tourism".

It is appropriate to mention about Indian doctors working abroad. Statistics indicate that around 60 000 Indian doctors are working in USA/Canada/UK/Europe/Australia. This is 10% of the registered physicians in India. They are present mostly in English speaking countries. A few of them are job seekers and the remaining use higher studies to get a hold on the job market. Doctors in area are job seekers. Status and respect to the doctors are not equal to their European and American counterpart. They were treated more as medical assistants. Job seeking Indian doctors are bewildered when they come to know that their Indian qualification is not recognized in countries like UK, Australia and New Zealand. It will be a laborious task to study again to get the prescribed qualification. They end up as assistants in hospital laboratory, medical services, medical colleges and pharmaceutical companies. It was reported that in Australia a few Indian doctors were working as taxi drivers and security guards until they found a right break. Many Indian doctors grudge that they are overlooked or deprived of promotion and/or higher official status despite their qualification and hard work. Hiring of Indian doctors for foreign assignment requires government of India clearance which is governed by bilateral agreements. Otherwise many will be happy to take foreign jobs even if it is less honourable.

Indian doctors numbering 15000 faced immigration problem in UK recently. Despite having good opportunities in India many of them preferred to stay in Britain. Although their participation in the coolie trade is negligible they are however not exempt.

Doctors are not spared by the BPO business culture. Recent development in BPO is utilizing the services of doctors for examining the medical claims received by the insurance companies. It is not just the clerical work of processing medical claim with data entries. In this process doctors go into the details of the medical side of the insurance claim. All the top technology firms like Wipro, TCS and Patni Computers are into this business. Doctors along with nurses and paramedical staff are hired and are given the task of analyzing the medical claim and give their opinion on the nature and status of the ailment/decease/damage that justifies the claim. It will be a technical report for which the knowledge and experience in the medical treatment and medicine field is essential.

Hiring had already started and the current salary is around Rs. 30,000 to 40,000 per month. Experts in complicated areas like heart/kidney/brain are paid in lakhs per month. USA spends a few billion dollars every year for the healthcare of its aging population which is around 200 crores. This is a new money spinning business for the BPO operators who can afford to keep qualified physicians. This will be a welcome trend for many new medical graduates and doctors who are frustrated in the government and private hospitals. This is very attractive both in terms of money as well as timing. US timing of 7 PM to 4am will not be an issue. They feel that it is better than slogging in government hospitals.

Outsourcing the legal back office is now being slowly introduced. Law graduates are being sent to USA for learning and training to equip themselves with US legal systems and practices. This development will lead to creation of an army of Cyber Vakil Gumastas (clerks of the Advocates). The irony will be that the Gumastas will be more educated and better qualified than the Vakils in USA. It should not be a shock to find few MLs (Master of Law) in the crowd of Gumastas. Law graduates may prefer to take up the lucrative and easy jobs in legal BPOs (now called LPOs) rather than struggling alone in the complicated, crime ridden, politically interfered and bureaucratic Indian legal system. There are about 1750 professionals already in operation and the expected strength is likely to exceed 20,000 by 2015. The business in dollar terms is estimated to be one billion. More than 250,000 law graduates roll out every year from various universities. Development of this business will lead to the introduction of study of American Law in many law institutions. Government of India appears to be showing receptiveness to the demand by UK and USA to open up the legal profession for them. This is pposed by the various Indian law associations which demand reciprocity. More than 50 legal consultants from USA had already opened their offices in India and brought in their back office operations like documentation, report preparation, and legal transcription. Indian judiciary is already struggling to solve the 50 lakhs cases pending in courts all over India. The new wave of law graduates will work only to help USA in clearing their back logs and they will be of little help to Indian judiciary which is in dire need of qualified professionals and infrastructure facilities.

Indenture within India is spreading to other industries also. This is called KPO (knowledge process outsourcing) which traps the talents in the fields of design, animation, technical writing, editing, preparing technical and financial analysis for various industries like engineering, medical, finance, and media, environmental and so on. Top line consulting companies from USA and Europe have established their offices in centers like Chennai, Bangalore and Mumbai. They hire well qualified financial, engineering, graduates, pay them very attractive salary and use them to do all analytical and research based assignments for their clients.

CHAPTER 24

Entry and Fortification of East India Companies

The latest move by the MNCs is to acquire the local call centers and BPOs and bring them under their direct control and supervision. This will strengthen their position and relieve them from the dependency on local firms for cheap labour supply. Recently IBM acquired a BPO Company Daksh with its 6000 employees. Citicorp took over E Serve International, a successful BPO having 4500 employees servicing customers in 20 countries. Genpact, promoted by General Electric of USA is a BPO with around 20000 employees located in 5 different cities in India. Wachovia Banking Corporation, a top US financial institution had already outsourced more than 75% of its back office to India. Office Tigers in Chennai run by an American manager has 1500 employees working 24 hours catering to the financial information needs of US Security & Exchange commission and leading investment bankers. The Chennai office has 50% of its total global workforce of 3000. 24/7 Customers P. Ltd., a US BPO has 6000 employees in its Bangalore office. Most of the assignments are to cater to the needs of customers located in different parts of the world. Convergys, another US BPO has a strength of 10,000 in India servicing all the daily needs of different customers spread out in many cities of the world. They have plans to add another 3000 more in the next 3 years. Lehman Brothers, a leading investment bank from USA had leased 25000 sq ft of office space in a prime location in Mumbai at an exorbitant rent. They may be shifting their back office to Mumbai. UK and US publishing companies have over 2000 employees in Bangalore engaged in designing, editing and proof reading all their books on various subjects. Accenture, a BPO company of Arthur Anderson has 19000 employees in their Bangalore office.

US and European MNCs must be wondering how they are able to get the required talented and cheap labour without any exertion. Twenty years ago campus interviews were generally done by well established Indian and foreign corporations, who looked for dynamic youngsters for managerial positions. Select institutions like IIT, BITS, Regional Engineering colleges and reputed B schools were the target of the corporations.

This trend had undergone a sea of change in the last five years. Almost all private engineering colleges and private B schools virtually beg technology corporations to visit them and conduct campus interviews. Universities have started conducting job fairs to attract more students. Job fairs have become very common in major cities. Thousands of young graduates gather in a playground to get more information about various jobs. This is similar to crowd gathered in sea ports to embark on ships sailing to South Africa, the Caribbean and Far East in the 19th century. These kinds of carnivals are visited by agents (Kankanis) of big corporations and they select bunches of graduates having BA/B.Sc/B.Com/MA/M.Sc/M.Com/MBA/ and MCA degrees suitable to their needs. Every carnival invites not less than 20,000 aspiring graduates. Stampede and rude elbowing in the disorganized crowd is a common scene. The scene is like the traditional wholesale vegetable or cattle market convened at the outskirts of towns.

Nasscom, in its web site published the following remarks of top line CEOs about India's potential to provide quality labour. Nasscom was very proud in publishing the remarks and projected India as a great tech. country. The CEOs are interested only in the POTENTIAL of low cost labour available and not the technological skill of Indians. Their statements clearly reveal how pleased they are to find the required labour at rock bottom price. Between quality and cost more weight is given to the later.

Above statements are very similar to the remarks made by the European and American Generals and Field Marshals of the first and Second World War praising the Indian contribution to their victory over Germany and Japan.

Statistics reveal that India is becoming the best servant USA ever had. India boasts of having more than 300,000 software engineers and rolling out 60,000 every year. The Indian government has realized the great opportunity of servicing the needs of the West. Every year the government has been liberalizing its restrictions on the foreign companies who are now looking at India as the best market to get cheap labour, which will increase their productivity and profit without spending for additional capacity. State governments are competing with each other to attract the giant computer firms like Microsoft, Dell, Motorola, Cisco, Intel, Nokia, and others. Andhra Pradesh took the lead in soliciting foreign investments, followed by Maharashtra, West Bengal and Tamilnadu. It is surprising that West Bengal, a communist dominated state for 5 decades is also after the Technology firms of USA. The Chief Minister of West Bengal visited USA to market his state for multinationals' investment. He was reelected as chief minister despite visiting USA the citadel of capitalism with a begging bowl. The truth is that the IT educated Bengali youth found Bangalore as their destiny to make their living. Bengalis who were in the forefront fighting the British imperialism and exploitation are reluctantly realizing the fact that the

Global Business Leaders are Bullish on India's Potential

(courtesy: nasscom.com)

Jack Welch
General Electric

"A truly global company will be one that uses the intellect and resources of every corner of the world.India is a developed country as far as intellectual capital is concerned.The opening of (offshore) development centres mark a new level of commitment by GE in india."

John Chambers,
CISCO Systems

"We are expanding our presence in india to take advantage of the ample research and development talent available...our Global Development Centre is a critical component of our future success."

Michael Dell,
Dell Computers

"India can become a major part of Dell's operations and a major source of the human capital that Dell takes on as a company... and we are looking for further opportunities to take advantage of skilled labour."

Bill Gates,
Microsoft

"Three years ago,during my visit to india,the country was emerging as an IT superpower. Today,the country is handling the most sophisticated projects in the world...I am impressed with the talent we have in our India Development Centre and the quality of software being developed."

Lawrence J Ellison,
Oracle Corp

"I love Indian food and only a few minutes away from my house in Redwood Shores is Gaylord where I eat a lot of naan, dal makhani and baingan bartha. Oracle is committed to India and has invested huge amounts of money in engineering. Yes, symbols are important for other top CEOs like Gates, John Chambers and Carly Fiorina have come to India, but I am deeply committed to the Indian venture where we have 2000 employees, which we will scale up to 4,000."

imperialists are more capable of creating jobs than the Desis. Educated Bengalis are pouring into Bangalore. The number of Bengali associations in Bangalore swelled from 2 in 1995 to 16 in 2005.

Central and state ministries are inviting MNCs to start their operation in their area of interest. They are lured by various concessions in taxation, social, financial and environmental requirements. Their presence is also used for political propaganda. A few Indian states are very considerate with MNCs in granting lands for their plants and factories. There are unconfirmed reports but strong rumours that State Government ministers in the pretext of encouraging MNCs to start their plant are now indulging in making millions for them and their party by allotting lands at unreasonable prices with mutual benefit for both. Lands are acquired by government order for a meager sum and allotted to the establishment and expansion of MNCs. In a few states, the land owners were coerced to sell by the threat of government acquisition. This is similar to the Maharajas and Nawabs who were generous in leasing lands to East India Company's activities. Grabbing of thousands of acres of arable lands in Bengal and Bihar by the British and European merchants for their indigo cultivation during the 19th century is now returning back to India in a different style. The Indigo commission of 1860 AD revealed the incidents of police and magistrates taking sides with the greedy European traders in their torturous pursuits of land grabbing. State governments with the assistance of centre are doing the job for the modern East India Companies.

Government in the centre seems blindly following the Chinese method of creating SEZs (Special Economic Zone) without proper plans and vision of future. SEZs are becoming a money making machine for the ruling parties. Kickbacks and camouflaged transactions are common in any government run either by democracy or despotism. It is reported that for a few SEZs the proposals are put forward after ensuring the adequate benefits for the ruling parties and their officials. Both central and state governments seemed to be grossly overlooking the social and environmental repercussions. Politically, economically, socially and geographically India is not China. Competing with China in the creation of SEZs needs more careful analysis. Western media is trying to provoke India by flattering China and its rapid economic growth precipitated by permitting western industries and business. Their media regularly indict rather ridicule at India's inability to match with China. Commerce and Finance ministries seemed to be in a hurry to finalise and implement as many SEZs as possible in the shortest possible time. It has two distinct advantages; (1) they earn the admiration from the western media and (2) a good opportunity to have control over free flow of funds, land acquisitions, lucrative contracts and a few more. SEZs are becoming a nightmare for poor peasants. If proper education and counter values are not provided to the peasants repetition of Santhals' rebellion can not be ruled out.

Nasscom reported the following statistics (Indiainfo.com dt. Nov/16/06). It is an indication of slow and steady expansion of MNCs into our cheap labour market.

Genpect	19700	employees
Accenture	19000	-do-
IBM Daksh	10000	-do-
E Serve (Citicorp)	NA	(about 5000)
Wipro (Indian)	12900	
ICCI (Indian)	8000	
HCL (Indian)	7500	

The top 4 positions in terms of number of employees are with US Corporation. Rough estimate of BPO employees in India is around 415000 and this figure is likely to swell up to 600,000 by 2008. As the present government had opened up its gates for the foreign corporations, they no longer need a local BPO company to cater to their needs. They now can create their own centers without any local assistance. Very soon the

BPO business will be cornered by MNCs as they have the financial muscle, management ability and brand name to cut into the markets of Indian BPOs. They have more information and much wider idea about the big potential of outsourcing business. Their worldwide operation can easily grab many opportunities coming to India in the BPO business. IBM, Citigroup and Accenture are more known to the developing regions like Middle East and Central Asian countries. Infosys, TCS, Sathyam and Wipro do not have the adequate government support to venture into new developing countries. Technologically backward Middle Eastern countries like Saudi Arabia, Kuwait, Jordan, and Egypt which are politically dominated by US will always prefer an American corporation even if they are expensive. US corporations will bag the orders from these countries and outsource it to their operation in India to increase their margins. US MNCs will be able to muster over two lakhs of cyber coolies in the next couple of years either by organic expansion and/or by acquisition. Indian youth like the youth of 1830 AD who showed more interest to join the East India Company force than the army of local Kings would prefer to join a BPO run by foreign MNCs. US and European governments give strong support to the operations of their own corporations. It is only a matter of two or three years whereby the foreign MNCs will be able to control either directly or indirectly more than 70% of the labour force required for their needs. Arm twisting contract terms are already in place to squeeze the medium and small Indian BPOs. US and European master are insisting on stringent conditions favourable to them in terms of pricing and termination rights. MNCs might eventually annex all the rights and privileges of hiring cheap labour for themselves. Britain did this before during the colonial days regarding supply of raw materials and this time its close associate USA will do the job but the product will be cheap and efficient labour pool.

The Government might be indirectly encouraging the foreigners to take over and control the cheap labour supply, which may restrict the big cry of the Left to unionise the new industry. Stage had reached whereby the foreigner need not have any local partnership or affiliation for their operation in India. The foreign based BPO and call center companies have since steadily increased in number and as usual they will be able to attract the best lot of the labour force. They are generally free from local political and social interference. They have the clout and influence to be above the social and regional requirements of states like quota for locals and backward class (SC/ST). They also have financial and managerial muscle with a strong backup from their governments to subdue the local giants. The best example is the growing domination of the big four chartered accountants, KPMG, Price Waterhouse, Ernst & Young and Deliotte Haskins & Sells. Leading Indian chartered accountant firms of the yester years are now taking sub-contracting jobs for these 4 firms. Top line Indian firms partnering with the big 4s will be dwarfed soon and become silent partners. Independent Chartered Accountants will be indirectly controlled and managed by the big 4 and in future they might become their hired professionals. The Government of India took sides with the big 4 in their pursuit to control the auditing and accounting profession in the country. Government advised the nationalized banks to insist on audit of their big borrowers accounts by the big 4s. This is indirect coercion in the name of globalization and liberalization. Bombay Chartered Accountants Journal reported that the total revenue (audit and consultancy) earned by the big 4 amounts to Rs. 2165 crores which is at least 8 times more than the combined revenue of all the registered Indian CA firms operating in India. A veteran Chartered Accountant expressed his doubts about their clear legal status in India, core business and the billing methodology with their local partners. It is only a matter few months when all of them will be set free to do their business independently. US government is planning to use the secrecy and privacy rule as a conduit to bring all Indian BPOs handling US transactions to be examined or audited by the big 4 audit companies to ensure maintenance of American standard of secrecy. Already few practising Chartered Accountants have taken up jobs like customer verification for credit cards and other financial verification services for consumer loan processing. It should not be a surprise even if our top 4 technology corporations end up with the same fate.

The danger is making the educated labour force more dependent on the activities of MNCs. Social scientists, eminent educationists and elderly scholars in India are very much worried that although the new wave brings extra money, it will drain the talent pool of the nation. A brilliant engineer lured by the high salary in BPO or Call center will never be able to use his knowledge and skill for future engineering and non software technological development. Thousands of engineering graduates, Chartered Accountants and students of professional courses are taking up IT related jobs. Chartered Accountants will be reduced to accounting clerks, law graduates will become cyber gumastas, MBAs will be limited to compile data and write analysis, graduates and post graduates of arts and science will be fit only to be BPO assistants or delivery boys. As mentioned before Good salary, attractive perks, holidays abroad, foreign assignments, generous bonus and ultra modern working conditions can easily deskill the talented workers. The wave of research works coming into India from abroad will snatch the best of the lot plunging Indian research capabilities into darkness.

The Average Indian will feel proud of the present importance given to Indians but he/she fails to realize the fact that these jobs can be done by Americans in USA but they are not so important to be handled by high cost American labour. There is no difference between the blacks of the 19th century and the browns (Indians) of 20th century. Indians cannot feel superior to the blacks just because they know mathematics and hold MBA or B.Tech degrees. USA needed the blacks from Africa in the last century to pick cotton in cotton fields and to dig in the coal mines now they need the browns from India to compile data and compute programs in the computers. It is just a matter of the need of the time. The status of both is same. The West had fully realized the potential of getting cheap and efficient labour. The Indian government has also realized the potential of getting foreign exchange and creation of employment opportunities. Presently it may be termed as a win, win situation for both; I am fine and you are fine. This scenario is not perpetual as every Indian dreams of it as being ever lasting. The West would have already made several contingency plans to coerce Indian government on this new development. They may not in future make requests to get their work done. Demands will be the next course of action. The Treasury Secretary of USA who visited Delhi in the last quarter of 2005 made a veiled statement that USA will not pull out the service providing business from India. The message is clear that they can and will pull out if they want. A self deluded Indian who thinks that USA cannot survive without the service of India will receive a rude shock when such an eventuality takes place. Indian workers' monopoly in Gulf was broken by cheaper labour from Philippines, Indonesia, Sri Lanka and Bangladesh; the same might happen for the technology boom also. It is not sure whether the Indian chambers of commerce, business guilds and labour/commerce ministries have any contingency plans to confront and manage a critical situation that may be created if USA takes an adverse stand. This may be unlikely in the near future but could easily be converted as trump cards to cajole rather threaten India.

The present situation is more or less closer to the political game played by The East India Company. The Subsidiary Alliance introduced by Lord Wellesley (1797 – 1805) was able to bring the numerous Maharajas and Nawabs under the East

India Company's indirect control. The British manned troops, under the subsidiary alliance, were stationed in princely states to protect their sovereignty against invaders and in return they bore the entire expense of the troops, which was twice costlier than desi troops. Many times the Indian rulers ceded part of their territory to the East India Company if they faced cash shortage to meet the expense. A British officer remarked "subsidiary alliance is a system of fattening allies as we fatten oxen, till they were worthy of being devoured". A similar situation in a different form and style involving labour cannot be ruled out in the future as we are opening up the country unscrupulously for foreign investments and exploitation of our labour.

USA played this game in a different way in Latin American countries particularly in Brazil. USA poured investments and started mega projects by using their political and financial mite. Brazil was unable to withstand the speed and size of the development plans. In ten years time it ended up with a burden of huge internal and external debts and an inflation rate more than 500% (!). Brazil, a country with vast natural resources plunged into debts and poverty in most parts of the country.

Robert Clive has returned to India in style. He did not have to waste his time and energy fighting the French, the Dutch, the Portuguese and the Moghuls. All his past European enemies are now his friends and partners; they also extend their co-operation in his pursuit to enforce the economic colonial rule in India in which they have a share. Indian government, this time had invited Robert Clive with a bouquet and red carpet.

CHAPTER 25

Dynamite Under the Dream

The side effects of fast growing employment opportunities are slowly becoming visible. The cheap labour is likely to result in cheap quality of performance. Mass recruitment in universities and colleges will always have 40% of the student force either less qualified and/or less suitable for the jobs for which they were selected. This is similar to the coolie brokers of the last century who were retained to send agricultural labourers, gathered and shipped anybody who fell in their net including carpenters, cobblers, roaming orphans, barbers and even beggars. Nasscom is already worried about the declining quality of our performance in BPOs flooded by raw graduates from rural areas who are unable to catch up with international standards. It is trying to introduce an industry standard to ensure quality and reliability.

The attrition rate in BPOs and call centers are as high as 25% which is mainly due to the heavy pressure from inside as well as outside the office. Young boys and girls enjoy their jobs inside their office, once they come out they face the typical Indian realities like, water problem, electricity cuts, traffic jams on the roads, crowding in places for leisure, entertainment and worship, government bureaucracy, political and labour strikes and civil commotion for silly reasons. Their life back home is equally stressful like their jobs. Working women suffer the most, as they are involved in domestic management also. Stress both inside and outside make their life miserable which in turn reflects on their poor quality performance. Exit interviews of big companies clearly indicated the work-life imbalance. Top line companies give more importance to this problem and are working with consultants for better solution. Our big 4s (Infosys, Satyam, Wipro and TCS) had been adding around 8000 (average) employees every year for the last 3 years; 25% represents replacements. This indicates that they are hiring more than 20 a day after interviewing at least 60 prospects. TCS had hired more than 20000 employees during the year 2005/06. The human resources department must be over working with 50% staff more than its normal requirement. What about the middle and lower level IT companies? They are in trouble even with 10% attrition rate. State governments generally run by selfish politicians and lethargic bureaucrats, take little interest to improve infrastructure facilities.

A leading US based but Indian managed technology company remarked that the quality of service is declining due to the attrition rate, yet the cost benefit of having the operation in India is still prevailing over the decreasing quality. Cost of Indian operations is on the increase as revealed by the big 4s who had been increasing the annual salaries by 10 to 15% for the last 3 years. India will become unattractive once the increase in cost and decrease in quality starts pricking the minds of the western masters. A few small US based technology firms in Bangalore are so frustrated by the high labour turnover that they had decided to close down and shift their operation outside India. They will have to find a better place than India to reconcile with cost benefit and quality. Countries like Malaysia, Thailand, Indonesia, Vietnam and Sri Lanka may be on their agenda of alternative sources.

Indians should realize that other nationals will also develop knowledge in English and mathematics and become our competitor. It is only a matter of 3 to 4 years when others can match us in knowledge and offer cheaper. Vietnam is a fast emerging BPO center. Intel Corporation invested $600 million for its chip development project. Microsoft, Sony, Nortel and Alcotel-Lucent are all setting up their new technology centers in Vietnam. Though South East Asian countries are far behind India in this business, they are developing fast and may emerge as our competitor. US corporations are also eyeing Mexico, Romania and Russia as their future venues for outsourcing

The present employment boom will decline after some time due to many economic and social pressures. Steady increase in urban cost makes top line companies to spread out to under developed areas. Cities are being categorized as tier I, II and III in the order of infrastructural facilities and availability of qualified labour, Politicians are very eager to develop technological parks in their area for political and economic reasons. First they get a political mileage for having brought in employment opportunities and second they can make a fortune as the investment value runs into several hundred millions of rupees.

IT companies will face a politico social trap after some time. One of the main reasons for encouraging investments in tier II and III cities is to provide employment opportunities to the thousands of graduates rolling out every year from hundreds of colleges around the cities. A politician openly made a remark that future IT parks should be in the interior parts of the state so that the graduates living in and around the area will have the employment opportunity. This approach is no doubt very logical but the social and labour problem will emerge once the employers try to import outside talent for development and improvement. If the top positions are predominantly occupied by outsiders it precipitates resentment from the lower level locals. Locals will have a stronger bargaining power as they enjoy the majority of the work force backed up by regional social and political forces.

An IT company which looks for 100% quality in order to survive in the international market will find it very difficult to chew the lesser quality service or product produced by the local labour. An Indian holiday resort company in the early 1980s started very well matching the service quality and management ability of any multinational company in the industry. Their holiday resorts in many hill stations were a great success due to hiring professionals from various parts of India. They, over the years, went down drastically in quality service and management due to persistent interference from local authorities. This kind of problem is inevitable for Indian companies in rural areas and they have no other alternative than to accept them. Our rural industrialization is far below the expected rate of development due to this problem. Foreign MNCs who look forward to high quality may not accept to set up in interior regions unless they get a substantial advantage. They will be able to get the best talents only from the cities. India is unable to get over this kind of social problem. Both emerging Indian and existing foreign MNCs will have no other alternative than to shift their operation to other countries where they will have freedom to bring in talents and free from localization pressure.

Privacy is part of the western culture and also one among the fundamental rights. Governments are under obligation to protect the privacy of individuals. Rules and regulations are very strict in safeguarding the privacy particularly relating to finance. Infringement of privacy and secrecy are generally punishable with hefty fines running into millions of dollars. India, although has privacy rules copied from the West, its record of maintaining it, is far below acceptable level. It is still not accepted as a general rule even by the educated Indians. This makes private information vulnerable to reckless exposure. It is very easy to get private information from the banks/insurance companies/stock brokers about their clients. There are no hard and fast rules preventing leakage of sensitive information. The West is really worried about the loose and ineffective control on infringement of privacy as BPOs in India handle millions of sensitive information about individuals/ corporations/societies/business houses/ health information/ insurance claims/ salaries/claims/ compensations/ technical formulas. Except one or two minor cases, the current situation is under control however the fear of leakage still daunts the West. Nasscom had come up with ideas to protect the secrecy of sensitive information but its implementation is a big task. A single incident of a serious breach of privacy will put a big dent on the credibillity of India.

There is a tax holiday of ten years for all BPOs started in 1999 that will end in 2009. The definition of a BPO eligible for tax holiday is still not clear. The Left parties are pressing for imposition of tax while the foreign BPOs are pushing for extension of another ten years from 2009. USA and European companies are known for their tax evasion techniques. They forced many small island states to become their tax heavens. Imposition of tax by the government may have adverse effect on this business. If it becomes less economical along with inadequate quality of performance the foreign BPOs will be forced to look for alternative countries. India will face a catch 22 situation.

India's share of the global BPO business is only 6%. India however enjoys the status as the leading offshore outsourcing centre. Statistics indicate that our share in this business is increasing at a diminishing rate. Many countries in Far East, Eastern Europe, South Africa and China are fast emerging competitors. Our commanding position is likely to become shaky in the near future.

CHAPTER 26

Indian Technology Tycoons

What are the achievements and standing of Indian software companies in the technological world? Are they really capable of protecting the interest and enhance the creditability of India? The investigation reveals disappointing information. Indian software and technology giants stand nowhere near the American multinationals in developing and making patents of the discoveries. India stands far behind even compared to China and Korea. IBM received more than a billion dollar every year from licensing its patented products, HP (Hewlet Packard) received around $ 200 million a year. Almost all the top line technology and communication MNCs like Nokia, Sun Micro Systems, and Oracle have several of their products patented. Unfortunately our big 4s are miserably lagging behind. The number of patented tech products of Indian origin is less than 100. Although the process of getting a product registered as a patent is lengthy and cumbersome, The Economist magazine (UK) points out that Indian company are not keen on this progressive path. Most of the Indian companies (95%) are involved in providing services to their US and European customers and have least interest in developing their R&D. An analyst remarked that Indian companies do more D than R. The D stands for development and/or delivery. The reputation is that they are both developing managers as well as delivery boys.

A survey by The Economist unfolded an interesting piece of information. The Indian big 4s are deliberately not registering their discoveries as it may create a competitive situation with their customers, which may eventually disturb the relationship. The most popular among the big 4s developed an automated system for one of its clients in the aero industry which cut the time by more than 70%, yet they did not want to register their new discovery but retained it as a closely guarded secret and using it for other customers in the same industry. The reasons for this approach could be (1) more revenue could be generated by keeping it as secret instead of revealing it to the world by registering them as patents (2) Indian government has still not come out with a system of registering patents for technology products, as of now technological innovations are not patentable in India. (3) Our government has absolutely no control on infringement of patents and illegal duplications. High ranking officials and peoples representatives are involved in producing/distributing spurious and duplicate products. Spurious Pepsi and Coca Colas were produced all over the country. State governments reported to have unearthed at least 10 cases of spurious cola factories in the last 10 years. Report from European Union indicated that 31% of the fake drugs discovered in different European cities are from India. Software piracy is another bug which cannot be controlled easily, particularly in India. Pirated versions are freely available even for sophisticated programs. Nasscom and BSA recently made a request in news papers not to use pirated versions of soft wares and also warned of a fine upto Rs.2 lakhs with 3 years imprisonment. They also announced a reward of upto Rs. 5 lakhs for exposing and reporting piracy. India is in the 301 priority watch list of USA. The 301 watch list consists of countries not providing required protection to copyrights, patents and other intellectual property rights (IPR). Patents can however be registered in USA. A few Indian tech firms have registered their findings in USA.

Following is the graph reported by The Economist on the patent registration in the technology sector.

India does not figure at all in the above graph. Are our IT giants happy and satisfied to be only delivery boys?

Company	*Number of patents*
IBM	40,000
Hewlet Packard	25,000
Microsoft	10,000
Intel	10,000
Nokia	12,000
Qualcom	1,800

Economist also hails that a US $ 6.5 billion revenue earning Huawei Technology of China has 34000 employees and 50% of them are involved in R & D. Even Chinese tech companies have more than 1000 patents registered and earn huge amounts in licensing their products whereas Indian counterparts make the junk of their revenue from providing various kinds of services.

Sample R&D expenses of few US corporations and their Indian counterparts.

Name	*R&D Expense As % of Total Revenue*
IBM	6.41
Microsoft	14.86
HP	4.02
Intel	13.24
Cisco	14.47
Oracle	12.63
Tata Consultancy	0.28
Infosys	NA
Wipro	0.52
Sathyam	0.04

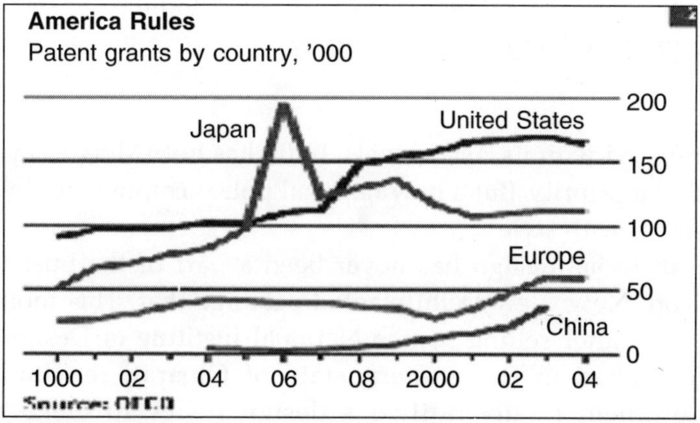

Courtesy: Economist.

A study of the income statement of the big 4s shows an encouraging surge of 83% in total revenue for the last three years whereas their R&D expenditure is meager compared to their US counterparts. The argument is that the big 4s are service and/or solution providers and not innovators. It is reported in Yahoo Finance that 25% of Wipro's revenue comes from the outsourcing of R&D work of Sun Micro Systems, Cisco and Intel.

The big Lament in the media by economic and technological experts to improve our innovative skills is a clear admission of the fact that Indians are capable of doing a given job perfectly. Except "Yoga" (physical exercise with emphasis on breathe control) there seems to be nothing in the international market as India's exclusive brand name. India is exposed to the world economic competition only in the last 10 years. It earned the reputation as an efficient service provider and accumulated huge amount of foreign exchange.

Future honourable survival for Indian MNCs depends more on their ability and drive to attract the world market with their innovative products.

Business week online (Feb/14/07 by Nandhini Lakshman) had produced an interesting survey.

Quote

Compared with its Asian rivals, India has been slow to make design a priority. But a new national policy commits to doing business with style

In India, design has never been a part of the business lexicon. Now, New Delhi wants to change that. This month, 40 years after setting up the National Institute of Design in Ahmedabad in the western state of Gujarat, the Indian government finally ratified a design policy to make the discipline a national priority.

To achieve this, the new policy envisages a "platform for creative design development, design promotion and partnerships across many sectors, states, and regions for integrating design with traditional and technological resources."

Not only has the NID been deemed a university, the government wants to set up four more NIDs and make design a part of the curriculum in engineering and other educational pursuits. Finer details are still scarce, but with education as the key issue, it will bank on public-private partnerships to foster design.

Design Latecomer

So far, India has only a dozen design programs, compared with 241 in China. There are 300 design colleges in Korea, in contrast to India's 10. While China churns out 30,000 design students annually, India produces just one-third of that number. And while Asia is increasingly becoming the hotbed of design, India is nowhere on the scene.

This policy is the first sign that the government wants to rectify that. It comes at a time when both China and India—with their roaring economies—are among the most happening destinations globally. Says Sridhar Marri, head of the communication design group at Infosys Technologies, "The design-led economic transformation that we have always dreamed of in India can now be visualized on the horizon."

This initiative would put an emphasis on innovation at all levels. Even as Japanese and Korean brands consistently give their western counterparts a run for their money, Indian brands continue to dominate only in their home market. But with Indian companies increasingly displaying global aspirations, the realization that only innovation and design can set them apart from the crowd is dawning.

Crucial Differentiator

"This is a great move from the government of India to express and indicate support for India's design and innovation capabilities in the global arena," says Niti Bhan, a San Francisco-based emerging-markets strategist. "If India takes a leaf from the other Asian nations' books, they have a chance to be catapulted onto the world stage."

Until now design has never been a big concern, but more an incidental function in Indian business. But today, with stiff competition and scores of foreign brands and services invading India, design and product offerings are being touted as the only differentiators in the clutter. "The policy has the power to create an innovation ecosystem in the country," adds Marri.

Driving this system are hordes of small and midsize enterprises that are using design to make their presence felt. Drawing on the vastness of India, with all its cultural diversity, marketers are using design to make a global foray.

Making It Click

Take the case of the Lexi pen, made by a small manufacturer. It has a cap that makes a satisfying click sound when it's shut. With the click denoting the preservation of the object, the pen has been a roaring success in India. Manoj Kothari, founder of Pune-based Onio Design, which designed the product, claims his client is set to launch this product overseas, with certain tweaks. But he adds, "Most of our design has been reactionary rather than preemptive."

And such instances are few and far between, as India is struggling to develop its own Samsungs and LGs. Kothari also points out flaws in the policy—a lack of practical application pointers, for one. "The generic vision statement has a Utopian bonanza built into it. What's missing is a sustained and integrated plan for design and innovation," he says. He compares it to a patchwork of swatches from different world baskets that have been sewn together. "We are using design as a noun, but it should be also a verb for systematic innovation."

At the very least, the policy is an indication that design and innovation are topics at the tables of the nation's leaders.

Unquote

Above write up should open the eyes of Indians and the government of India on how they are lagging behind even in Asia. It is time the Indian MNCs gather their resources and strength and apply them to implement a strong and effective long term policy on innovation and patent rights.

Recently Indian software and engineering companies registered patents in India and USA. It is reported that over 14000 patents were registered during 2007-08. This is only the beginning of a long road ahead. There are impregnable political, social, economic and traditional forces, in the country that can easily destablise the enforcement of patent rights. Patent rights should not become a mere paper certificate.

There is no point in blaming our technological giants. They are all capable of competing with top tier US and European firms. They have the credit of pioneering the concept of Indian MNCs. They lack the government support in labour, finance, taxation, global expansion and local amenities. They are also unnecessarily dragged into local labour, political and social conflicts. Bureaucrats and politicians grudge their development and growth instead of assisting them. Politicians are disappointed with their inability to exercise influence over them as the market and major operations of these giants are outside India. Few ministries do take steps to provide facilities but they are slow, less efficient and inadequate. Pampering the top brass with awards, titles and frequent media coverage may not be of much help in making them global giants. Our big 4s are relatively small compared to their rival MNCs in terms of financial strength, market size and global presence. They are vulnerable to take over by big fish from USA/Japan/Europe.

Globalisation had become irreversible and it is time that full co operation is extended both from public and government to Indian MNCs before the foreign MNCs take control of our trade and commerce. They should be given all assistance and encouragement to use the globalization drive for their expansion and development internally and globally. They should not become Maharajas of the colonial days enjoying life under the supervision of The British. The onus is on the people and government of India. The Government of India should strengthen their economic diplomacy at the international level and encourage emergence of many more Indian MNCs.

Finally a self pitying statement, If the government of India and the dominant political parties underestimate the corporate power houses of USA and Europe and fail to take good care of our MNCs, they may be swallowed up by their foreign competitors. Eventually India will be again run by a few modern East India Companies; this time they may be from USA instead of the UK.

Conclusion

The present wave of economic activities generating thousands of employment opportunities together with growth in the housing sector and consumer durables is not generated by us. It was underwritten by multinational corporations of USA and Europe who shifted many of their routine back office jobs to low cost areas like India and China. The New Economic International Order (NEIO) is a cry from developing countries particularly from India that rich and affluent countries must help the poor by sharing some of their wealth and income by reforms in the international system. The rich and dominant should help the poor nations with minimum income generating capabilities to face the economic hardships. This is termed as "Mini-Income Targets". Henry Kissinger remarked that "International co operation must be directed to the problems of creating a secure basic economic security for all and this challenge is above ideologies and block politics. No international order can be considered just if co operation with the aim to raise the poorest of the world to a decent standard of living is one of its basic principles". The present boom we are now enjoying is a kind of aid program under the 'Mini-Income Targets".

> "All progress at the dictation of another is valueless in my opinion."
>
> —*Swami Vivekananda*

Both India and China are developing themselves into being inevitable for the western corporate world. China gets manufacturing and India gets service providing. How long this boom will last is a difficult question to answer now. Local pressure to prevent shifting jobs to low cost areas in USA and Europe is still strong. John Kerry, the Democratic rival of George Bush put in his election manifesto that he will stop or at least discourage jobs moving out of USA to India. Had John Kerry won the presidential election, the present boom would have been much slower than what it is now. There are bills both in the US congress and individual states waiting to be tabled prohibiting transfer of jobs to India and China. There is a website called "No jobs to India.com" which propagates stopping jobs shift to India.

Our freedom fighting leaders struggled for 90 years and set the country free from all bondage. The 33 years from 1947 to 1980 was the period of pride and determination. We could not sustain ourselves as independent people for long. We are politically independent but economically not, because of our own inefficiency and ignorance. World is emerging from industrial era to information era. World economy is taking a rapid change by eliminating border limitations. Borderless economy is fast spreading in Asia and MNCs from USA and Europe are taking full advantage of the new development. We have been branded and exploited as the efficient service providers, meaning servants. We were servants during the agricultural era and industrial era; our status continues to be the same in the current information era. We emerged from British Raj to Swaraj and now we are in Noukar Raj (Country of Servants).

Leo Tolstoy, the famous Russian thinker and novelist asked Mahatma Gandhi in his letter "Letter to a Hindoo" "A commercial company enslaved a nation comprising of two hundred millions. Do not figures make it clear that it is not the English who have enslaved the Indians, but the Indians have enslaved themselves"? The above statement is a bitter truth about India's past. Are we committing the same mistake again and going back to square one.

Articles, news clips and statements are appearing in various business magazines, and newspapers that R&D is shifting slowly to Asia from USA, particularly to India and China. The media and various writers are spreading a dream that in future all technological innovations will be generated from India and the West will be at the receiving end. Mao Tse Tung the great communist leader who unified and ruled China for 3 decades did the same propaganda called "a great leap" in 1960. He spread the dream to the Chinese that China will become the leading industrial country beating UK, Germany and USA. His dream did not materialize until the West started investing in China by shifting their manufacturing operation, again to take advantage of cheap labour. India's recent tech boom is also built up on the same structure.

Low profiled and oppressed sections in societies are getting a new name and trying to gain recognition. The nominal respectability by way of change of name granted to sex workers and African Americans is also extended to accounting clerks, Munshis, secretaries, enquiry clerks hardware/software mechanics (!) who are now known as data operators or service providers and knowledge workers. The recent GDP figures indicate that 55% of GDP is from service sector (inclusive of transport) There is every possibility that 75% of the 55% (GDP) is to cater to the needs of customers who are neither Indians nor Indians abroad. Economic projections reveal that 75% of our export income will be generated by service sector pushing down the industrial and trading sectors. The garden coolies of the 19th century toiled in the sugar, tea, rubber plantations to service the confectionery, automobile and beverages/alcohol industries in UK and Europe. Indian cyber coolies now toil day and night to lower the cost and improve the productivity of the western MNCs. Have we really changed from 19th century? Will we change and start a new era from this boom? God only knows. We can sell only the best available with us and that is the ability to serve obediently for others, probably that is the will of God. ***Dasan may be the destiny of desis.***

APPENDIX 1

Source: Google Books— Book of George Somoult Fagan

The Act XXI of 1844 initiated by Lord Stanley was the beginning of Indian indentured labour which subsequently took a new name as NRIs (Non Resident Indians) and POI (People of Indian origin). The first batch of Indians numbering 236 to British Guyana had grown in 160 years to 20 million (2 crores) NRIs and POIs.

While writing several pages of criticizing the exploitation of Indian labour by western corporate powers one should not forget or neglect the rules and regulations enacted and enforced by western governments in providing the proper care and compensation to the hired workers from foreign countries. Rights of workers such as minimum compensation amount, safety and security in workplace, health and accident insurance, decent work place, extra compensation for over time work, secure transport to work place, annual leave, service end benefits are all ensured. The Emigration Act of 1844 had prescribed several conditions for the export of Indian labour. It was to ensure that slavery is not re introduced. Strict vigil was in place on the agents of labour suppliers who were termed as "man merchants". Emigration of Indian labour was suspended several times during the period 1864 to 1908 due to deaths during the harsh voyage, unsuitable living and working conditions and ill treatment by the colonial masters. A Magistrate was stationed at all ports of emigration. All workers had to declare that they are going at their own will and not under any threat or coercion. Man merchants were to be registered with the government for the supply of labour; ship captains are authorized to take only the labourers certified by the agents. All registered agents were required to submit a report every month. Ship captains were warned with hefty fine ranging from Rs. 200 to Rs. 5000 if they indulge in smuggling of Indian labourers for the colonies. Customs Officers were empowered to search the ship and its records to make sure that illegal labour trade is not undertaken. There were conditions on safe voyage and the ration eligibility for the workers going abroad to work in plantations. (Appendix 1, 2 and 3 gives details of these conditions)

Although many of the regulations were violated by the western masters, the sufferings of the workers were reported and government action was taken in many cases. In the case of H1B visas issued by USA conditions regarding minimum decent compensation to all the foreign workers were strictly enforced. This was not the case in regard to workers hired in Gulf and South East Asian countries. Western masters insist on adequate compensation and decent work place for all the workers employed by Indian companies who perform the BPO functions for their Western principals. Although cheap work places are available they wish to maintain a minimum standard. The recent change in the more decent and technically advanced work place culture even among Indian companies is due to the influence of the growing American work culture in India.

Act No. XXI of 1844

1. Partially Repeals Act XIV, 1839.
2. Laborers, natives of India, to be allowed to emigrate to Jamaica, British Guiana, and Trinidad from Calcutta, Madras and Bombay.
3. Presidency Governments may appoint as Emigration Agents at each port the nominees of the Colonial Governments. Agents to report monthly.
4. Presidency Governments may nominate a Protector of Emigrants at each port.
5. No Vessel to carry emigrants without license, but grantity of license to be discretionary. Fee to be not more than one rupee per emigrant. Master to enter into a bond in duplicate to conform to the conditions of this Act.
6. Emigrant laborer not to be received on board without a pass from be Agent countersigned by the Protector.
7. Emigrant Vessel not to obtain Port Clearance without Certificate from the Emigration Agent.
8. The probable lengths of voyages from the three ports to the three colonies; Emigrant Vessel to sail only between 30th September and 1st March.
9. Before Port Clearance granted, Master to deliver to the Emigration Agent a list of the emigrants on board and obtain from him a counterpart.
10. Penalty of Rs.200 per emigrant on Master of Emigrant Vessel learning out without previous compliance with requirements of this Act.
11. Penalty of Rs.500 for every emigrant taken on board and not entered in list and counterpart.
12. Penalty of Rs.5,000 besides forfeiture of bond, for doing or allowing any fradulent act whereby the certificate becomes in applicable.
13. Officers of Customs to have same powers of search and detention for evention of the illegal embarkation of emigrants as for prevention.

(14,15, 16 not available)

17. Penalities to be enforced or by putting in suit the Master's Bond.

Schedule 1. Nomination of Emigration Agents. 2. Remuneration to be by salary. 3. Duties. 4. Properties of passengers to tonnage, height between decks. 5. Children how to be reckoned. 6. Provisions. 7. Provisions and water to be surveyed before clearance. 8. Provisions to be supplied for forty-eight hours after arrival. 9. Copies of regulation. 10. List of Emigrants to be delivered to Agent and counterpart to Protector. 11. Admiralty Vessels and Ships of war excepted from the Act.

An Act for regulation the Emigration of the Native Inhabitants of the territories under the government of the East India Company of Jamaica, British Guiana and Trinidad.

I. Partially repeals Act XIV. of 1839—It is hereby enacted, that Act No. XIV. of 1839, and all Acts repealed thereby, so far as the same are applicable to the Emigration of Natives from the ports of Calcutta, Madras and Bombay respectively, to Jamaica, British Guiana, and Trinidad, are repealed. Provided always that the aforesaid Act No. XIV of 1839, shall remain in full force in all the ports of India, except the ports aforesaid, and in regard to Emigrants from India proceeding to other places than Jamaica, British Guiana, Trinidad and Mauritius.*

II. Emigration to be allowed to Jamaica, British Guians, and Trinidad from Calcutta Madras and Bombay—And it is hereby enacted, that, after the passing of this Act, Emigrant Labourers, being Native inhabitants of the territories under the government of the East India Company, shall be allowed to pass and to be conveyed to Jamaica, British Guiana, and Trinidad respectively, from the ports of Calcutta, Madras and Bombay respectively, but not otherwise.

III. Government may appoint Emigration Agents at each port. Agents to report monthly.—And it is hereby enacted, that at each of the three ports aforesaid, it shall be lawful for the Government of the Presidency within which the port is

* See Acts VIII of 1857 and IV. 1852 by which respectively emigration to the Mauritius is permitted under Act XV of 1842, from the ports of Madras and Bombay as well as from that of Calcutta. By Act XLIX. of 1860, this Act is to be taken to refer to Act XV. 1842, as amended there by as to supply of water.

situated, to authorize such persons as may be nominated by the Government of Jamaica, British Guiana or Trinidad, to act as Emigration Agents at the aforesaid ports respectively, and to exercise the powers conferred on Emigration Agents by this Act, and every such Emigration Agent shall make monthly Reports to the Government, to which he is subordinate, of all matters transacted by him in pursuance of this Act.

IV. Government may nominate a protector of Emigrants at each port.—And it is hereby enacted, that at each of the three ports aforesaid, it shall be lawful for the Government of the Presidency within which the port is situated to nominate a proper person to act as Protector of Emigrants at the aforesaid ports respectively.

V. No Vessel to carry emigrants without license. Fee to be not more than one rupee per emigrant. Master to enter into a Bond in duplicate to conform to the conditions of this Act.—And it is hereby enacted, that it shall not be lawful to convey any Emigrant, being a Native of India, who may embark for the purpose of laboring for hire in any of the Colonies of Jamaica, British Guiana or Trinidad from any of the ports aforesaid in any ship or vessel, unless a License be obtained for carrying Emigrants in such ship or vessel from the Government of the Presidency in which the port is situated. A fee, not exceeding One Rupee per Emigrant, as may be regulated from time to time by the local Government, shall be demandable in respect of every such License, which fee shall be carried to the credit of the said Government, and the granting or withholding any such License shall be entirely discretionary with the Government, and in consideration of such license the Master of every ship conveying or destined to convey Emigrants from India, shall execute a Bond binding himself and his owners in a penal sum of 10,000 Rs. to conform to the several conditions herein provided, and the said Bond shall be executed in duplicate, that it may be put in suit either at the place of execution or in the Colony to which the

Emigrants are to be conveyed, and one copy shall be forwarded to the Government of such Colony, to be dealt with as the case may require. And every ship or vessel in which any such Emigrant shall be conveyed without a License being obtained as aforesaid, shall be liable to be forfeited, and the Master thereof shall be liable, as for a misdemeanor, in a fine of 1,000 Rupees for every such Emigrant so illegally conveyed.

VI. Emigrant to be received on board without a pass counter signed.—And it is hereby enacted, that it shall not be lawful for the Master of any vessel licensed as above to receive on board any Emigrant laborer, as above provided, unless such laborer shall have in his possession and show a Certificate or Pass, to be given to him by the Emigration Agent of the port, countersigned by the Protector, stating his name, and the name of his father and his age, and certifying that having appeared before such Agent, he has declared his willingness to proceed to work for hire in the Colony to which such vessel is bound, and has been engaged by him as an Emigrant to such Colony on the part of the Government thereof.

VII. Emigrant Vessel not to obtain Clearance without Certificate.— And it is hereby enacted, that before any ship or vessel, so licensed to carry Emigrant laborers as above provided, shall be cleared out from any of the aforesaid Ports for any one of the three Colonies aforesaid, it shall be necessary for the Master of such ship or vessel, provided any Emigrant of the description aforesaid shall embark therein, to obtain from the Emigration Agent so nominated and authorised at such port as aforesaid, a certificate under the hand of such Agent to the effect following, that is to say.

1st—That such Agent has, by personal communication, done what is required on the part of such Agent by the 3rd Article of the Schedule hereunto annexed; provided always, that every such Agent shall make the inquiries specified in such Schedule in an open Court or public office to which all persons shall have admission.

2dly—That all the directions contained in the 4th, 5th, 6th and 7th Articles of the said Schedule for ensuring the health and safety of passengers have been duly complied with.

3rdly—That (in addition to the directions contained in the said Schedule) such rules have been complied with, as the Governor-General in Council shall from time to time frame, touching the medical attendance and medical stores and the proper clothing to be provided, the species of provisions suited to Native habits, the number of women that should accompany the Emigrants, or other matters.

VIII. The probable lengths of voyages; Emigrant Vessel to sail only between 30th September and 1st March.—And it is hereby enacted, that the probable lengths of the voyages to Jamaica, British Guiana and Trinidad from the Ports aforesaid respectively shall, for the purposes of this Act, be deemed to be—

For the Port of Calcutta, twenty weeks;
For the Port of Madras, nineteen weeks;
For the Port of Bombay, nineteen weeks;

and that no ship or vessel carrying Emigrant laborers to Jamaica, British Guiana, or Trinidad shall sail from Calcutta, Madras or Bombay, at any other time than between the 30th day of any September and the 1st of March next thereafter ensuring.*

IX. Before Clearance, Master to deliver to the Agent a list of emigrants on board and obtain from him a counterpart.—And it is hereby enacted, that, before any ship or vessel shall be cleared out from any of the aforesaid ports for Jamaica, British Guiana or Trinidad, it shall be necessary for the Master thereof to deliver to the Emigration Agent, so nominated and authorized at such port as aforesaid, the list

* Repealed, as to Emigrants Vessels sailing from Madras, by Act XXV, 1845, Sec.2, and as to Emigrant Vessels sailing from Calcutta by Act IV, 1852, Sec.2. The 31st August is substituted in each case for the 30th September.

specified in Article 10 of the said Schedule, and to obtain such duplicate thereof as is required by the said Article.

X. Penalty on Master, clearing out without previous compliance with requirements of this Act.—And it is hereby enacted, that if the Master of any ship or vessel shall, at any of the ports aforesaid, take on board such ship or vessel any Emigrant laborer of the description aforesaid, and shall clear such ship or vessel for Jamaica, British Guiana or Trinidad, without having fully complied with every particular herein before required previous to clearance, he shall be liable, on conviction before any Magistrate or Justice of the Peace, in a penalty of 200 Rupees for every Emigrant laborer so taken on board his ship or vessel.

XI. Penalty of Rs.500 for every emigrant not entered in list and counterpart.—And it is hereby enacted, that if the Master of any ship or vessel shall, after having cleared such ship or vessel at any such port as aforesaid for Jamaica, British Guiana or Trinidad, take on board any such Emigrant laborer as aforesaid, without having entered such Emigrant laborerin such list as aforesaid, or without having obtained such duplicate as aforesaid, containing the entry of such Emigrant prior to clearance, he shall be liable, on conviction before any Magistrate or Justice of the Peace, in a penalty not exceeding 500 Rupees for every Emigrant so taken on board his ship or vessel.

XII. Penalty for doing or allowing any fraudulent act whereby the certificates becomes inapplicable.—And it hereby enacted, that if any Master of any ship or vessel cleared for Jamaica, British Guiana or Trinidad as aforesaid shall, after having obtained such Certificate as aforesaid, fraudulently do or suffer to be done any act or thing whereby such Certificate shall become inapplicable to the altered state of the ship or vessel, its passengers or other matters to which such Certificate relates, such Master shall be liable on conviction in any penalty not exceeding 5000 Rupees, beside incurring a forfeiture of any

Bond executed in consideration of any license obtained for the vessel as originally described.

XIII. Powers of search and detention for prevention of the illegal embarkation of Emigrants.—And it is hereby enacted, for the greater security against Emigrant laborers being embarked for Jamaica, British Guiana or Trinidad, contrary to the provisions of this Act, that all the powers vested by law in the Officers of Customs in regard to the searching and detention of Ships or Vessels, or otherwise for the prevention of smuggling on board thereof, may be exercised by such officers for the prevention of the illegal embarkation of such Emigrants as aforesaid on board ships or vessels bound for Jamaica, British Guiana or Trinidad, and of other offences against this Act; and it is further enacted, that all Pilots in the service of the East India Company shall be invested with the same powers and be charged with the same duties as Preventive Officers of Customs in this behalf.

XIV. Penalty for exporting any native contrary to the provisions of this Act.—And it is hereby enacted, that every person who shall attempt, by means of intoxication or by false imprisonment, or other means of crimping, to export any Native on board any ship or vessel contrary to the provisions of this Act, shall be liable to be punished, on conviction before a Magistrate, in a fine not exceeding 500 Rupees, or imprisonment not exceeding six months; Provided, that nothing in this Act contained shall prevent the offender from being proceeded against by indictment, but the offender shall only be liable to one of these courses of proceeding.

XV. Customs Officer to countersign each pass and to keep a register of Emigrants on board, and not to leave the vessel till after muster made in his presence, and that of the Pilot, Customs Officer and Pilot both to report to the Agent. Penalty for false report of connivance.—And it is hereby enacted, that whenever a vessel shall clear from Calcutta for Jamaica, British Guiana or Trinidad with Emigrant laborers duly embarked thereon, the Customs Officer on board such vessel shall countersign the Pass or Certificate brought on board such vessel by every such Emigrant laborer, and shall keep a Register of every such Emigrant laborer as may come on board. And such Customs Officer shall remain on board such vessel until she shall arrive in Saugor Roads, and shall not come away until muster of the Crew and Passengers and Emigrant laborers has been made in his presence, and in that of the Pilot in charge of the vessel; and after the Customs Officer has taken muster and quitted the Vessel, the Pilot shall continue to exercise the duties indicated in Section XIII of this Act; and it shall be lawful for him, if he shall deem it necessary, to require the Master or Commander to take a general muster of the Crew and Passengers and Emiogrant laborers on board and to sign a muster roll so taken, and every such Custom House Officer and Pilot shall make a complete Report of the Emigrant laborers on board of any ship at the time of his quitting the same, and such report shall contain a declaration that, to the best of the declarant's belief, no additional Emigrant laborers have been received on board since obtaining the Certificate, and that nothing else has been done or omitted to be done in the ship or vessel contrary to the provisions of this Act; and every such report or muster, if any, shall be transmitted without delay to the Emigration Agent of the Port. And any Custom House Officer or Pilot who shall wilfully make a false, erroneous or incomplete Report of the Emigrant laborers on board of any ship, or who shall connive at the unauthorized embarkation of any such Emigrant laborers, shall be liable, besides dismissal, to a fine of 500 Rupees, commutable, if not paid, to imprisonment in the Calcutta Jail for six months, and the penalty shall be adjudged in like manner as similar penalties are adjudged for offences committed in respect to the Customs Revenue.

XVI. Penalty for forgery of documents requires by this Act.—And it is hereby enacted, that if any person shall forge, or shall use, knowing it to be forged, any document required by this Act, such person shall be liable to be imprisoned for any period not exceeding seven years.

XVII. Penalties to be enforced by information or by putting in suit the master's Bond.—And it is hereby enacted, that all the several penalties to which the Masters of ships or vessels are liable by this Act, shall be enforced by information laid before any Justice of the Peace at the instance of the Emigration Agent, or of any officer appointed for the purpose by the Government of the place or Presidency, or may be enforced by putting in suit the Bond given by the Master, if such Bond has been given in consideration of the license granted to the Ship.

SCHEDULE

1. Nomination of Emigration Agents.—The Governors of Jamaica, British Guiana and Trinidad may from time to time nominate such persons as they shall see fit, to act as Emigration Agents at Calcutta, Madras and Bombay.

2. Remuneration to be by salary.—The remuneration to be given to any such Agent in India shall not depend upon or be regulated by the number of the Emigrants sent by him, but shall be in the nature of an annual salary.

3. Duties.—Every such Emigration Agent shall ascertain, by personal communication with every Emigrant previously to his or her embarkation from the port, or place for which such Agent shall have been appointed, that such Emigrant has not been induced to emigrate by any frand, or false or unreasonable expectation, and is aware of the distance of the Colony to which he or she is about to emigrate, from the place where he or she is about to embark; and such Agent shall explain the real advantages likely to be derived by such Emigrant from a removal to such Colony, at the same time cautioning such Emigrant against unreasonable and unwarrantable expectations; and such Agent shall also

ascertain that every such Emigrant is in good health, and not incapacitated from labor by old age, bodily infirmity, or disease.

4. Proportion of passengers to tonnage. Height between decks.—It shall not be lawful to ship on board of any ship or vessel, carrying Emigrants from India to any of the Colonies aforesaid, any number of passengers exceeding the proportion of one person for every two tons of the registered burthen of such ship or vessel, and no such ship or vessel carrying Emigrants, and having more than one deck, shall have less than the height of six feet at the least between decks; and in case such ship or vessel shall have only one deck, a platform shall be laid beneath such deck, and in such manner as to afford a space of the height of six feet at the least, and that such platform shall not be so laid as that the lower beams shall project above the same, and that no such ship or vessel shall have more than two tiers of berths; and that no such ship or vessel shall carry Passengers on any such voyage to any of the Colonies aforesaid, unless there shall be an interval of six inches at least between the deck or platform and the floor of the lower tier throughout the whole extent thereof; and, whatever may be the tonnage of the ship or vessel, no greater number of Passengers shall be taken on board of such ship or vessel than shall be after the rate of one such persopn for every twelve superficial feet of the lower deck or platform unoccupied by goods or stores, not being the personal luggage of such person.

5. Children how to be reckoned.—In the computation of the number of Passengers within the meaning of these Regulations, two Children under the age of ten years shall be considered as equal to, and shall be reckoned as, one person only.

6. Provision.—There shall be actually laden on board of every ship or vessel, conveying Emigrants into any of the Colonies aforesaid, at the time of departure of such ship or vessel from the port or place at which such laborers shall be embarked, good and wholesome provisions for the use and consumption of the said Passengers, over and above the victualling of the Crew, to the amount or in the proportion following, that is to say-a supply of water to the amount of five gallons for every week of the computed voyage for every Passenger on board such ship or vessel, such water being carried in tanks or sweet casks, and a supply of rice, bread, biscuit, flour, oatmeal, or bread stuffs to the amount of seven pounds weight to every week of the computed voyage, for every such Passenger; Provided always, that, when any such ship or vessel shall be destined to call at a port or place in the course of her voyage, for the purpose of filling up her water casks, a supply of water, at the rate before mentioned, for every week of an average voyage to such port or place of calling, shall be deemed to be a compliance with this Regulation, and provided that the preceding Regulation regarding food shall be deemed to have been complied with in any case when it shall be made to appear, that, by the special authority of the Governor-General of India in Council, any other articles of food were substituted for the articles above enumerated, as being in his judgment equivalent thereto.

7. **Provision and water to be surveyed before clearance.**—Before any such ship or vessel shall be cleared out on any such voyage, the Agent appointed for the port or place from which such ship or vessel shall be cleared out, shall survey or cause to be surveyed by some competent person, the provisions and water hereinbefore required to be on board for the consumption of Passengers, and shall ascertain that the same are in good and sweet condition, and also that over and above the same there is on board an ample supply of water and stores for the victualling of the Crew of the ship or vessel, and shall also ascertain that such ship or vessel is generally reputed sea-worthy, and that the directions hereinbefore contained for ensuring the health and safety of the Passengers

have been complied with, and shall grant a certificate thereof under his hand to the Master of such ship or vessel.

8. Provision to be supplied for forty-eight hours after arrival.—The Master of every ship or vessel conveying Emigrants to Jamaica, British Guiana or Trinidad shall be bound to provide for and furnish to every such Emigrant, and his wife and children, a sufficient quantity of good and wholesome Provisions for his, her and their daily maintenance during such voyage and during the space of 48 hours next after the arrival of such ship or vessel at the place of destination.

9. Copies of regulation.—Two copies of these Regulations, authenticated by the signature of the Agent at the port or place at which such Emigrants shall embark, shall be delivered to the Master by such Agent on demand at the time of clearance, and shall be kept on board of every ship or vessel carrying such Emigrants as aforesaid, and one of such copies shall, upon request made at reasonable times to the Master of the ship or vessel, be produced to any Passenger of his perusal.

10. List of Emigrants to be delivered to Agent and counterpart to Protector.—The Master of every ship or vessel carrying Emigrants from India to any of the three Colonies aforesaid, shall, before clearing out such ship or vessel, deliver to such Agent at the port or place from which such vessel is cleared out a list in writing, together with a duplicate of the same, specifying as accurately as may be, the names, ages and occupation of all and every the Emigrants on board such ship or vessel, and such Agent shall thereupon deliver to the said Master the counter-part of such lists, signed by such Agent, and the said Master shall on the arrival of such ship or vessel at the place of destination, and previous to the disembarkation of any such Emigrants, give notice of the arrival of such ship or vessel, and deliver the said counterpart of such list to the Protector of Emigrants appointed, or to be appointed, at the Colony at which the said Ship or Vessel may have arrived.

11. Admiralty vessels and ships of war excepted.— Provided always, that nothing in these Regulations contained shall apply to any ship or vessel in the service of the Lords Commissioners of the Admirally, or to any of Her Majesty's Ships of War.

ACT No. XXII. of 1844.

Repealed by Act XIII. 1862.

APPENDIX 2

1. Contract

This Charty [*sic*] Party of affreightment, made this ______ day of ______, 184 ______, by and between ______, [hereinafter referred to as the "Party of the first part,"] as Secretary to and on behalf of Her Majesty's Colonial Land and Emigration Commissioners of the one part, and ______ of ______ [hereinafter referred to as the "Party of the second Part,"] for and on behalf of the owners of the Ship ______, mentioned and described in the foregoing tender, of the other part. WITNESSETH, that for the considerations hereinafter mentioned, they the said Parties hereto of the first and second parts respectively, do hereby mutually covenant and agree with each other that they will severally observe, perform, fulfil, do, and keep, all and singular, the terms, agreements, stipulations, things, and conditions herein contained on their parts respectively to be observed, done, and performed.

2. Number of Emigrants

The said Party of the first part, hereby engages, that in case the said ship be placed at the disposal of the Government Emigration Agent at [hereinafter referred to as the "Port of Embarkation"] between the ______ and the ______, for the conveyance of emigrants to ______, there shall be put on board such ship and paid for the full complement of emigrants which by the law in force in India the Ship shall be qualified to carry, or if a smaller number be put on board, that payment shall notwithstanding be made for the full complement, Provided always, that in either case in respect of any emigrants who may die during the voyage, the amount of their passage money shall be deducted from the whole amount payable under this agreement.

3. Penalty, if Contract not carried out

And the said party of the first part further engages, that if from any unforseen cause, the Government Emigration Agent aforesaid shall be unable to supply the said ship with emigrants, and to employ her as intended by this Charter Party, then the said party of the first part, shall forfeit to the said party of the second part, a sum of two pounds ten shillings per register ton of the said ship, and the present contract shall be in all other respects void. Provided always, that if the said Ship does not arrive at the Port of Embarkation within the period mentioned in clause 2, it shall be optional with the Government Emigration Agent to employ her or not, accordingly as he may find that his other arrangements will admit, without the said party of the first part being liable to any penalty of damages whatsoever for not employing the said Ship.

4. Ships to go to India and be offered to the Emigration Agent

In consideration whereof, the said party of the second part hereby engages that the said Ship shall proceed to India, and make all due despatch on her voyage, and that after the discharge there of any Cargo or Emigrants that may be on board she shall not proceed in search of any other employment, but shall with the least possible delay be placed at the disposal of the Government Emigration Agent at the Port in India above named for the conveyance of Emigrants, and that in case of default in any of the said particulars the said Party of the second part shall forfeit and pay to the said Commissioners the sum of Two pounds ten shillings per register ton of the said ship, as liquidated damages, to be recovered with full costs of suit.

5. Ships to be Seaworthy and properly manned

And the said Party of the second part further agrees that during the continuance of this Charter Party the said Ship shall at all times be tight, staunch, strong, and substantial, both above water and below, and in all respects seaworthy, and properly and efficiently manned.

6. Fitments

That before any Emigrants are put on board under this Contract the said Ship shall, at the proper costs and charges of the said Party of the second part, be fitted in the between-decks with proper bed-places for the accommodation of the Emigrants to the satisfaction of the said Government Agent at ________, and shall also be fitted and furnished with proper masts, sails, yards, rigging, anchors, cables (two of chain), ropes, cords, apparel, and all other furniture fit and needful for the intended service, and shall also have a life-buoy, long-boat, two cutters, and a jolly-boat, a sufficient number of properly-fitted scuttles in each side, and such deck-light ventilators as may be required; suitable privies and also a separate hospital for males and females, head-pump, with sufficient tarpaulins, awnings, a windsail for each hatchway, and scuttle butts; and shall also at all times be furnished with sufficient scrapers, brooms, swabs, sand and stones for dry rubbing, swing stoves, and whatever else may be necessary for the cleanliness of the Ship and the comfort and safety of the Emigrants.

7. Emigrants to have use of Deck

That the whole of the space fore and aft between the decks, shall be appropriated and given up to the sole and entire use of the Emigrants, and that the upper deck, excepting the space occupied by the spare spars and long-boat, shall be kept quite clear for their use.

8. Victualling and Medicines, &c.

That in case any Emigrants shall be embarked in the said Ship under this Contract, there shall be on board provisions and stores for their use during the voyage of a quality to be approved by the Government Emigration Agent at the Port, and equal in quantity to Twenty weeks' consumption, if proceeding from Calcutta, and Nineteen if proceeding from Madras, calculated according to the annexed, or any other not more expensive scale to be settled by such Government Emigration Agent, for the numbers that may be embarked; and also a supply of Medicines and Medical Comforts according to the annexed, or such other not more expensive list as may be determined on by the Government Emigration Agent as aforesaid. The Medical Comforts to be issued at the discretion of the Surgeon, whether for the sick, or to preserve health.

9. Water

That the Water shall be of the best quality that can be obtained, and be approved by the Government Emigration Agent, and shall be put in sweet and substantial casks properly charred, and constructed of staves of at least one inch in thickness for the ground tier, and not less that three-quarters of an inch for the remainder.

10. Surgeon

That there shall be provided at the charge of the said Party of the second part a duly qualified Surgeon, to be approved by the said Commissioners or by the Government Emigration Agent at the Port of Embarkation to take Medical charge of the Emigrants during the voyage.

11. Good treatment of the Emigrants

That the said Emigrants shall be treated with kindness by the Master, and all the Officers and the Crew of the said Ship; and that the Master shall on all occasions, when practicable, attend to any suggestions of the Surgeon calculated to promote the health, comfort, or well-being of the Emigrants; and, further, that the Emigrants shall on no occasion be called on to do any manner of work on board the Vessel other than cleaning their own berths between the decks, or receiving at the hatchways in the between-decks fresh water, and provisions and fuel; and that on the occasions of cleaning their berths they shall on no account be placed to draw water from the sea on the gunwale, in the chains, or in any situation which shall endanger their falling overboard.

DIETARY SCALE FOR EMIGRANTS FROM INDIA TO THE WEST INDIES

The following is to be the Scale for one Adult. Women to receive the same as Men; Children between One and Twelve to receive one half. No ration for Infants under One year.

Dholl	4 [ozs.]
Ghee	1 [oz.]
Salt	1½ [ozs.]
Turmeric	1 [oz.]
Onions	1 [oz.]
Tobacco	1 [oz.]
Chillies	1/2 [oz.]
Tamarind	2 [ozs.]
Firewood	4 lbs.
Salt Fish	4 ozs.
Water	3/4 gallon per day.

Dry Provisions for bad weather when the usual Provisions cannot be cooked.

Choorah (Avil)	1 seer, or 2 lbs.
Bhootgram (Cuddalay)	1/4 seer, or 1/2 lb.
Sugar	1 cuttack, or 2 ozs.

Eighteen days' stock of dry Provisions to be laid in for the voyage.

LIST OF MEDICINES AND MEDICAL COMFORTS

Supply for any number of Emigrants, from 50 to 100. The quantities to be increased for any additional number beyond 100, at the rate of half these quantities per 100.

	lbs.	*ozs.*
Acacia Gum		6
Acetate of Lead		3
Adhesive Plaster	1	4
Alumen		6
Antimonial Powder		2
Aromatic Spirit of Ammonia		8
Blistering Ointment	1	8
Blue Pill		4
Carbonate of Ammonia		3
Camphor		6
Cerate (simple)	1	8
Chloride of Lime	4	8
Calomel		6
Castor Oil	4	8
Compound Tincture of Camphor		8
Dover's Powder		3
Epsom Salts	2	
Extract of Colocyunth		3
Ginger Powder		6
Jalap ditto		4
Ipecacuan ditto		3
Nitrate of Silver		1/2
Opium		3
Oil of Peppermint		1/2

APPENDIX 3

Copy of Labour Contract for Mauritius (1836) (Source: wikiepedia)

Copy Form of Contract

Between the undersigned ______________ acting on behalf of ____________ of Mauritius, and the natives whose names are hereunto affixed, the following agreement has been entered into by the several parties binding themselves to the observance of the conditions thereof:

1. The natives agree to proceed to the Isle of France, to work as labourers there, upon a sugar estate, the property of ________________ and to remain there, if required, for the time of five years.
2. The passage of the natives to the Mauritius shall be paid by ______________who shall also provide a passage again to this country, at the end of five years, for each native who may then wish to return; but if any individual, from any cause, should be discharged or leave the employment of before the expiration of five years, such individual shall have no claim on him for a passage.
3. The pay of the natives shall be fixed at the rate of five rupees per month for each man. The labour required from them will be that of digging holes, weeding canes, working in the sugar-house, repairing roads and bridges, or otherwise making themselves useful, according to their ability, as may order them; the quantity of daily labour required from each to be fixed by the manager of the property; the pay of one sirdar shall be fixed at seven rupees per month, and that of one mate six rupees, and boys at three rupees per month.

4. As _____________ must be responsible to government that the natives shall not be a burden to the colony, in the event of their being discharged or leaving their employments, one rupee per month shall be retained from the pay of each individual, until there shall be a sufficient sum to provide a passage for each to Calcutta; should no such contingency take place, the money shall be restored at the end of five years.
5. In addition to the pay as above fixed, food and clothing shall be supplied to each as follows — Fourteen chettacks of rice (about 2lbs.), two ditto of dholl*, two ounces of salt, and some oil and tamarind, daily; and annually for each, clothing as follows; two dhooties, two blankets, one jacket, and one cap.
6. Each individual shall receive six months pay in advance, for which he shall give an acknowledgement here; their pay to commence from the date of their going on board the ship.
7. The nature of this agreement (which shall be registered at the police) is such, that each native is individually responsible for the observance of its conditions by every one whose mark it bears; and it is further agreed, that while in hospital, from sickness or any other cause, the pay is stopped during such time.

* Something like dried split peas

Copy of Labour Contract for South Africa (1912)

The Indenture Agreement

The following is the indenture agreement of 1912:

1. Period of Service—Five Years from the Date of Arrival in the Colony.
2. Nature of labour—Work in connection with the Cultivation of the soil or the manufacture of the produce on any plantation.
3. Number of days on which the Emigrant is required to labour in each Week—Everyday, excepting Sundays and authorized holidays.

4. Number of hours in every day during which he is required to labour without extra remuneration—Nine hours on each of five consecutive days in every week commencing with the Monday of each week, and five hours on the Saturday of each week.
5. Monthly or Daily Wages and Task-Work Rates—When employed at time-work every adult male Emigrant above the age of fifteen years will be paid not less than one shilling, which is at present equivalent to twelve annas and every adult female Emigrant above that age not less than nine pence, which is at present equivalent to nine annas, for every working day of nine hours; children below that age will receive wages proportionate to the amount of work done.
6. When employed at task or ticca-work every adult male Emigrant above the age of fifteen years will be paid not less than one shilling, and every adult female Emigrant above that age not less than nine pence for every task which shall be performed.
7. The law is that a man's task shall be as much as ordinary able-bodied adult male Emigrant can do in six hours' steady work, and that a woman's task shall be three-fourths of a man's task. An employer is not bound to allot, nor is an Emigrant bound to perform more than one task in each day, but by mutual agreement such extra work may be allotted, performed and paid for.
8. Wages are paid weekly on the Saturday of each week.
9. Conditions as to return passage—Emigrants may return to India at their own expense after completing five years' industrial residence in the Colony.
10. After ten years' continuous residence every Emigrant who was above the age of twelve on introduction to the Colony and who during that period has completed an industrial residence of five years, shall be entitled to a free-return passage if he claims it within two years after the completion of the ten years' continuous residence. If the Emigrant was under twelve years of age when he was

introduced into the colony, he will be entitled to a free return passage if he claims it before he reaches 24 years of age and fulfills the other conditions as to residence. A child of an Emigrant born within the colony will be entitled to a free return passage until he reaches the age of twelve, and must be accompanied on the voyage by his parents or guardian.

11. Other Conditions—Emigrants will receive rations from their employers during the first six months after their arrival on the plantation according to the scale prescribed by the government of Fiji at a daily cost of four pence, which is at present equivalent to four annas, for each person of twelve years of age and upwards.
12. Every child between five and twelve years of age will receive approximately half rations free of cost, and every child, five years of age and under, nine chattacks of milk daily free of cost, during the first year after their arrival.
13. Suitable dwelling will be assigned to Emigrants under indenture free of rent and will be kept in good repair by the employers. When Emigrants under indenture are ill they will be provided with Hospital accommodation, Medical attendance, Medicines, Medical comforts and Food free of charge.
14. An Emigrant who has a wife still living is not allowed to marry another wife in the Colony unless his marriage with his first wife shall have been legally dissolved; but if he is married to more than one wife in his country he can take them all with him to the Colony and they will then be legally registered and acknowledged as his wiv.

APPENDIX 4

Detail of NRIs and PIOs all over the World

Country	*PIO People of Indian Origin*	*NRIs*	*Stateless*	*Total*
Afghanistan	500	0	0	500
Argentina	1200	400	0	1600
Australia	160000	30000	0	190000
Austria	3000	8900	0	7900
Bahrain	0	130000	0	130000
Barbados	2100	100	0	2200
Belgium	0	7000	0	7000
Bhutan	0	1500	0	1500
Botswana	3000	6000	0	9000
Brazil	1500	400	0	1900
Brunei	500	7000	100	7600
Cameroon	250	0	0	250
Canada	700000	150000	1000	851000
Cyprus	0	300	0	300
Czech Republic	20	400	0	420
Denmark	900	1252	0	2152
Egypt	40	1350	0	1390
Eritrea	30	1700	0	1730
Fiji	336500	250	0	336750
Finland	410	750	10	1170
France	55000	10000	0	65000
Germany	10000	25000	0	35000
Ghana	2000	1800	0	3800
Greece	0	7000	0	7000
Guadeloupe	40000	100	0	400100
Guyana	400000	100	0	400100
Hong Kong	29000	22000	0	51000
Indonesia	50000	5000	0	55000
Israel	45000	300	0	45300
Italy	36000	35000	0	71000
Jamaica	60000	1500	0	61500
Japan	1000	9000	0	10000
Kazakhstan	0	1150	0	1150
Kenya	85000	15000	2500	1021500
South Korea	200	2500	0	2700
Kuwait	1000	294000	0	295000
Lebanon	25	11000	0	11025

Country	*PIO People of Indian Origin*	*NRIs*	*Stateless*	*Total*
Libya	400	12000	0	12400
Madagascar	25000	3000	1000	29000
Malaysia	1600000	15000	50000	1665000
Maldives	0	9000	0	9000
Mauritius	705000	11200	0	716200
Mozambique	20000	870	0	20870
Myanmar	2500000	2000	400000	2902000
Netherlands	20000	15000	2000	217000
Nigeria	8000	17000	0	25000
Norway	0	5600	0	5600
Oman	1000	311000	0	312000
Panama	211	1953	0	2164
Philippines	24000	2000	12000	38000
Portugal	65000	5000	0	70000
Qatar	1000	130000	0	131000
Reunion Islands	220000	55	0	220055
Russia	44	16000	0	16044
Saudi Arabia	0	1500000	0	1500000
Seychelles	2000	3000	0	5000
Singapore	217000	90000	0	37000
South Africa	1000000	0	0	1000000
Spain	16000	13000	0	29000
Sudan	300	1200	0	1500
Suriname	150300	150	0	150450
Sweden	9000	2000	0	11000
Switzerland	8400	4800	300	13500
Syria	1800	0	0	1800
Taiwan	1800	0	0	1800
Tanzania	85000	5000	0	90000
Thailand	70000	15000	0	85000
Trinidad and Tobaco	500000	600	0	500600
UAE	50000	900000	0	950000
Uganda	7000	5000	0	12000
UK	—	—	—	1200000
Ukraine	0	3400	0	3400
USA	—	—	—	1700000
Yemen	100000	900	0	100900
Zambia	10000	3000	0	13000
Zimbabwe	15500	1200	0	16700

Figures for Sri Lanka is missing. The estimated Indian population which include nationals, rebels and stateless is around 3 million.

APPENDIX 5

Investment of MNCs in India

Year (April-March)	*Amount of FDI inflows (In US$ million)*
1991-1992 (Aug-March)	167
1992-1993	393
1993-1994	654
1994-1995	1,374
1995-1996	2,141
1996-1997	2,770
1997-1998	3,682
1998-1999	3,083
1999-2000	2,439
2000-2001	2,908
2001-2002	4,222
2002-2003	3,134
2003-2004	2,634
2004-2005	3,755*
2005-2006 (Up to March 2006)	5,549

An increase of 3222% in 14 years period.

Important sectors of the Indian Economy attracting more investments into the country are as follows: (as of close of 2005)

Industry	*US$ Mil*	*Ind Rs. Cr*
Electrical Equipments (Computer Software & Electronic)	4216	1686
Telecommunications (radio paging, cellular mobile, telephone)	2730	1092
Transportation Industry	3070	1228
Services Sector (financial & non-financial)	2840	1136
Fuels (Power + Oil Refinery)	2500	1000
Chemical (other than fertilizers)	1818	727
Food Processing Industries	1172	469
Drugs & Pharmaceuticals	936	373
Cement and Gypsum Products	715	286
Metallurgical Industries	544	217

Foreign investments in service sector and computer sector had substantially increased during the period 2006 and 2007.

Foreign technical collaboration approved by Government of India.

Country	*No of collaborations*	*% of total*
USA	1172	22
Germany	1106	14
Japan	868	11
UK	860	11
Italy	474	6
Others	2851	36

The intention of sanctioning the above collaborations is to ensure transfer of technology by which India will benefit in future.

The reality, however is to take complete advantage of government subsidies, cheap Indian labour and creation of trading bases particularly sea ports to cover other Asian markets. India is the cheapest country to have manufacturing base.

Countries that have Invested in India

Country	*US$ billions*	*Ind Rs. Crores*
USA	19.6	7840
UK	18.8	7520
Singapore	12.4	4960
Netherlands	11.5	4600
Japan	9.1	3640
Germany	6.4	2560
France	3.3	1320
Switzerland	2.9	1160
Cypress & Mauritius	107.0	42800 **

** Cypress and Mauritius are countries where big multinationals have their offshore centers. They establish as a local company and operate their international business from these centers to avoid tax obligations in their home country. These countries are small and economically backward. They depend on multinationals for funds and local employment. Their laws are deliberately kept very flexible and give good opportunities for multinationals. Investors from these countries are multinationals with a valid local registration.

APPENDIX 6

The Conclusion of the Book is Reconfirmed by our Prime Minister

Courtesy: Yahoo India News, dated August 26th, 2008

Guwahati, Aug 26 (IANS) India is expected to account for a fourth of the world's total skilled workforce by 2020 and the central government is according top priority to higher education, allocating Rs.275,000 crore (Rs.2.75 trillion) to the sector, Prime Minister Manmohan Ṣingh said here Tuesday.

'Our government's effort has been to create the next wave of investment in higher education. And the 11th Five Year Plan which is now under implementation is basically a knowledge investment plan,' the prime Minister said.

'We have significantly increased allocation to the education sector with a five fold increase to an unprecedented Rs.275,000 crore,' he said while addressing faculty and students at the Indian Institute of Technology (IIT) in Guwahati.

The prime minister said the government was trying to extend quality elementary education to all taking major expansions in secondary and higher educations. The idea was to produce some 500 million trained workforce by 2020.

Approval had already been granted for eight new IITs, seven Indian Institutes of Management, 16 central universities, 14 world class universities, five Indian Institutes of Science, 10 new National Institutes of Technologies, 20 Information Technology Institutes, and 1,000 polytechnics, he added.

'India has the potential to create over 500 million trained people by the year 2020. That would be over a fourth of the global workforce. This big and unique opportunity for India will come from an education revolution that we must undertake as our most important national endeavour.'

The prime minister also advocated the need for partnerships between ths state and the private sector to further boost higher education in the country.

'We need to work in close partnership with the corporate sector, non-governmental entities and community organisations. We need to facilitate creative partnerships between the public and private sectors in the field of education including higher education,' he said.

The prime minister, who then left for New Delhi ending his two-day visit to Assam, had to cancel his visit to the western Kokrajhar district Tuesday due to bad weather, officials said.

Chennai, Monday, April 2, 2007

'Around 20 companies participated in the job fair.'

Over 30,000 aspirants throng job fair at Madras University

Express News Service

Chennai, April 1

Youngsters queuing up at the job fair held at Madras University on Sunday —*Express*

MORE than 30,000 job aspirants thronged the two-day 'Career Fair 2007' which got underway at the University of Madras on Sunday.

The fair registered around 10,000 candidates in the first few hours after opening.

A similar Career Fair, was organised by the University along with Riddhi Consulting, last year too. Around one lakh candidates had participated in the fair at that timeAround 20 companies including HCL, Slashsupport, HTMT, Lason India, Allsec Technologies, Nittany and a few banks participated in the job fair. , of which only 1,500 candidates were recruited.

"Companies participating in the fair are cumulatively offering 2,000 jobs. Last year, Slashsupport had recruited around 300 candidates. We expect around one lakh candidates to visit us by tomorrow," said Jai Prabhu, managing director of Riddhi Consulting.

Graduates of all disciplines were eligible to attend the job fair. Online registry in Riddhi consulting's website was also available. Around 15,000 candidates had registered online.

"Through the online registry, we can maintain a database and circulate it to the companies. This will address to their future requirements too," he added.

The organisers had also arranged a separate test space for the candidates to take the aptitude test conducted by the companies.

On Sundays, head-hunters shortlisted 562 candidates for employment in BPOs, call centres and the publishing, sales and marketing industry. Of this, Slashsupport had shortlisted 95 candidates for its technical and customer support services, while Riddhi Consulting had 316 candidates. HTMT and HCL had shortlisted 35 and 40 candidates respectively. While 32 candidates were shortlisted by Lason India, Fullerton had 19 candidates. Allsec Technologies will conduct the second level of interviews on Monday.

Fresh offers will be available for candidates on Monday.

References

Chapter 1

K.M. Munshi, R.C. Mazumdar and D. Puslkar, *The Age of Imperial Unity.*

Chapter 2

K.S. Lall, *Muslim slave system in medieval India.*

Chapter 3

www.njashelsinkk.f1

African settlements in India by Abdulaziz Y. Lodhi, Upasala University, Sweden. Nardic Journal of African Studies.

www.anc.org

Indian Slaves in South Africa

Chapter 4

freeencyclopedia.com

Coolie- General/Regional usage

www.1911 encyclopedia.org

Coolie-Indentured Labour

www. Nationalarchives.gov.uk

Forced Labour a New system of slavery

www. Nationalarchives.gov.uk

Forced Labour a New system of slavery.

www.bbc.co.uk - 10.08.2005

Coolies: How Britain Reinvented slavery.

www.yahoogroupsglobaltamils 03.08.2004.

Diaspora. Setting the stage for Indian coolies abroad

Chapter 5
www.mversityofcalgary.com
The Nature of the Diaspora
www.himalmag.com
South Asian
Diaspora by Dhirupatel
www.ahfg.net
The Indian Diaspora
www.Indiana.edu
Indenture Labour letters between John Gladstone and messars, Gillanders Arbuthnot & Co.
www.Ucalgary.ca/applied history
Why indentured Labour

Chapter 6
www.infoplease.com
Guyana 1838 - 19.11.05
www.guyanaundersiege.com
Indian Indentured Immigration to Guyana - Hill Coolies
www. Manastheindiandiaspora
Freedom in chains indenture labour & Indian Diaspora in the Caribbean
www.guyana.org - 11.11.2005
www.jamaicaleaner.com
Pieces of the Past the Arrival of Indians by Rebecca Tortello

Chapter 7
www.southstseaport.org(southstreetseaport)
In The Kingdom of Sugar by Edwin G.Burrows and Mike Wallace.
www.indiana.edu
Indian Plantation Workers in Mauritius
www.himalmag.com
South Asian Diaspora Mauritius by Dhiru Patel

Chapter 8
www.rudyfoto.com - 13.02.2006
Indians of East Africa by Rudy Brueggermann

Chapter 9
www.newauthors.org.uk - 12.05.2004

The Coolies Doctor by Dr.Sathish Khanna,
www.aboutsouthafrica.com
A little known aspect of Indians - South Indians in South Africa.
www.rediff.com - 29.09.2004
South African Indians Prefer Apartheid
www.scnc.ukzn.ac.za
Arrival of Indians in South Africa-Pieces of the past by Dr. Rebecca Tortello

Chapter 10
www.hinduonnet.com - 10.06.2000
Frontline, The Indian Connection & Fiji Indians by Subhash-Singh.
www.fijiinstituteofappliedstudies.com
Girimitiyas : The Origins of the Fiji Indians
(Excerpts from The new book by Dr. Brijilal, Australian National University)

Chapter 11
www.immi.gov.au
Australia-Community Information Summary The India born Community
www.teapapa.gov.nz
Indians in New Zealand
www.sikh.com.au
Indians arrival in Australia-Sikhs in Australia
www.workpermit.com - 09.09.2005
Australia's rural areas want Indian immigrants
The New Indian Express - 28.08.2006
Australian Universities keen to take more India students
The New Indian Express - 20.09.2006
Paving the way for students to get passport to Australia
The New Indian Express 20.11.2006
India provides 25% skilled migrants to Western Australia

Chapter 12
www.chennaionline.com - 04.11.2005
Business-Record UK Visas for Indians
www.nrilinks.com
Indian American History

www.nriklinks.com
USA—Facts about Indians in USA
www.punjabonline.com
Pioneer Asian Indian Immigration to the Pacific Coast. Komagata Maru
www.nrilinks.com.usa
Indian American Community – History USA Indian achievements in USA Facts about Indians vs. average Americans.
www.wikipedia.indian diaspora.org
Non-Resident Indian and person of Indian origin in USA and Canada
www.punjabbonline.comimmigsration
Pioneer Asian Indian Immigration to the pacific coast chronology of immigration
www.alif.org
The Passage from India The Brief History of Indian Immigration to the U.S.
www.saxakali.com
East Indian in Canada's pacific coast 1900-1914 An encounter in Race Relations by Sahadeo Basdeo

Chapter 13

www.nmm.ac.uk
National Maritime museum Lascars-able Seaman
www.connections-exhibitions.org
The Impact of empire Lascars
www.blogger.com - 23.05.2005
The Lascars of old Hong Kong posted by Stephen and Dane
www.shipwrekwatch.com
First Known Wreck-Campbell Macquarie
www.fathom.com
The First Asians in Britain - The Demand Lascar labour. British Attitudes towards the Immigrant Community
www.portctres.org
Lascars in the East end
www.timepirates.attic.media.com
Items of interest at Royal Victoria Dock Lascars

Chapter 14

www.fathom.com

The First Asians in Britain—The Colonial Context Status of Indian British Society.
www.Indianresources.org - 23.09.2004
India Exporting Nurses to UK and USA
www.thehindubusinessline.com - 03.08.2002
US Hospitals Scouting for Indian Nurses
www.rediff.com - 16.02.2004
Indian nurses flock to the US
www.The British Library.com
Ayahs servants and sailors - Asians in Britain
www.Indolink.com
Studies Reveal Indian Nurses are Victims of Racism by Francis-Assisi
Dhinamani
Training Courses for Nurses going Abroad.
The Economic Times
US Congress has Reauthorised the Nurses visa Programme.
Breathing Space - Visa Window
Dhinamani - 14.01.2007
Info by Minister Vayalar Ravi
The Indian Express - 27.08.2006
Training Classes for Nursing Graduates

Chapter 15

www.littleindia.com - 13.02.2006
The Gujaratis by Lavina Melvani
www.prospectives.com - 20.05.2006
Diamond Business in Belgium
www.saxakali.com
An encounter in race relations by Sahadeo Basdeo.

Chapter 16

www.black-history.org
Black Information Link - World War One
www.littleindia.com
First World War - Belgium & France
www.atimes.com
Online Asia Times - Indian Soldiers lured by Dollar by Siddhartia Srivastava

www.memorialgatestrust.com
First world war-Mesopotamia
www.indianarmy.nic.in
Army History-Indian Army
www.bl.uk
British library-Asians in Britain and Indian Soldiers in World War
www.encatra.msn.com
Indian Soldiers in France.
www.cpiml.org
No Indian Troops to serve the US war in Iraq
www.wikipedia.org
World War 1 Causalities
www.bbc.co.uk
India and the western front by David Omissi
www.mgtrust.com.org
Participants from the Indian subcontinent in the first world war
www.bbc.com - 23.09.2004
Hitler's secret Indian army by Mike Thomson
www.memorialgatesstrust.com
The Memorial Gates on constitution hill (picture)
www.mgtrust.org
First world war-Belgium & France
www.British library.uk
Indian soldiers in world war
www.mgtrust.com
Second world war-North Africa
The New Indian Express - 24.11.2006
Army short of 12000, officers
Tradition of the army by Dharam Pal, National Book Trust
Dhinamani - 12.11.2006
Sonia pays tribute to the Indian soldiers died in first world war-her visit to Belgium.

Chapter 18

Dhinamani - 02.08.2006
Victims of Bahrain disaster paid 1.5 lakh to get the job
The New Indian Express - 01.08.2006
Bahrain Tragedy Victims in Distress
Dhinamani - 01.08.2006
Bahrain workers did not get four months salary

Dhinamani - 04.011.2006
Cheating by Promise of Jobs Abroad

Chapter 20

www.littleindia.com - 05.08.2007
Harish Trivedi Call center workers are the new Slaves Labourers of the 21st Centaury.
www.yaleglobal.yale.edu - 31.10.2005
Painful Truth of the call center cyber coolies - The Observer.
www.newstatesman.com - 10.11.2003
The Rise of the Cyber Coolies by Praful Bidwai.
www.rediff.com - 11.07.2003
It Experts or Cyber-coolies by Praful Bidwai.
www.epw.org - 31.01.2004
Cyber Coolies' in BPO. Insecurities and vulnerabilities of Non-standard Work by Babu P. Ramesh.
The Hindu - 17.01.2007
IT/ITES staff face insomnia problems
The New Indian Express - 13.12.2006
BPO employees have right to union, says ILO

Chapter 21

www.computerworld.com - 02.09.2003
It's Global Itinerary Offshore Outsourcing is Inevitable
www.outsourcing.com
Out Sourcing in India-Blog source
www.msnbc-msn.com
Outsourcing: Silicon valley East by Keth Naugthan
www.nasscom.com
Global business Leaders are bullish on India's Potential
The New Indian Express - 02.02.2007
CISCO Systems to Expand its Presents in India
The Economic Times - 12.12.2006
Dupont to set up R & D center in Hyderabad
The New Indian Express
More Workforces join the outsourcing Version
The Economic Times
Patni targets 15000, workers by year and/cognizant to add 12000 employees.
www.eweek.com - 22.02.2006

Outsourcing in India Pays on by Stan Gibson

Chapter 22
www.rediff.com/businessweekonline - 25.01.2006
Why outsourcing to India is a great Idea by Pete Engardio, Business Week.

Chapter 23
www.igate.com
Clinical Research/the India Advantage
www.en Wikipedia.org
Business Process outsourcing
The New Indian Express - 29.08.2006
India not a Guinea Big for Clinical Trials
The New Indian Express - 14.01.2007
India's Clinical Outsourcing Market to Grow Sizably
Dhinamani - 14.01.2007
Hundreds of Fisher Women Sell their Kidneys
The New Indian Express
Kidney Racket Thrives in Chennai
The Economic Times
CRO boom is a non-starter
The New Indian Express - 24.10.2006
Medical Transcription holds good Business Potential Business India
The New Indian Express - 17.09.2007
Asia's Latest Outsourcing Jaunt-Legal Services.
The Economic Times - 09.03.2007
Foreign Legal Eagles Fly to India
The Economic Times
Chennai base for MNC LPO Cobra Legal
Dhinaman - 17.11.2006
Americans Look at India for Medical Treatment
The Economic Times - 01.11.2006
Research Plan for Sankara Nethralaya
The New Indian Express - 23.10.2006
US Government Permit Medical Treatment in India
The New Indian Express - 17.11.2006
Engineering Services Outsourcing Next on Cards.
www.arunshourie.voiceofdharma.com

When SKY is the Limit by Arun Shourie
www.Indian Journal of Surgeons.com (Migration of Indian Doctors)

Chapter 24

www.indiainfoline.com - 16.11.2007
Infocus Genpact is No. 1 BPO in India
www.rediff.com - 05.12.2006
Thousands or BOP Jobs that Pay Big by Hidhi Sinha/Out Look
www.nasscom.in
Competitive Cost (Knowledge Professionals)
www.ecommercetimes.com
To Triple Investments in India
www.nasscom.com
Global Business Leaders Are Bullish on India's Potential. Strengths of India.
www.neweconomist.blogs.com
IBM's Massive Indian Expansion Poses Risks for its Competitors-Bloomberg
www.a-Bangaladesh.com
Indigo Commission
The New Indian Express - 06.03.2007
IBM Places India High on its Acquisition Radar
Dhinaman - 17.12.2006
Thousands (50000) Students gather in Job Fair
The New Indian Express - 13.11.2006
It is the time to go to fairs ... for jobs too
The New Indian Express - 08.03.2007
US Team Calls on Budha with Investments Bouquet
The Economic Times - 02.02.2007
IBM India nos. may swell to 120K by 2008
The Economic Times
Accenture to Ramp up India Headcount
The New Indian Express - 09.12.2006
Infosys Preparing to take on Accenture, IBM head-on
Dhinamani - 24.12.2006
Students should be keen to Join Manufacturing Sector-Emphasis by industries.

Chapter 25
The Economic Times
Attrition Rate Swells in Infy
The Economic Times
Convergys Grapples with High Attrition at all Levels
The Economic Times - 05.03.2007
BPO Industry will Collapse if Taxed as PE: Morgan Stanley
The New Indian Express - 08.03.2007
24 MNCs to Exit Indian BPO Industries
The New Indian Express
NASSCOM Announces Litmus Test for BPO job Seekers
The Economic Times - 21.12.2006
Patent nos Climb but Overseas Unimpressed

Chapter 26
www.theeconomist.com - 20.10.2005
Survey, Patents and Technology a Market for Ideas
www.dq-india.com
Intellectual Property.
Indian wakes up to patents by T.V. Mahalingam, Aug, 4, 2003
www.Yahoo Finance.com
Financials of IBM, Microsoft, HP, Intel, Cisco and Oracle
Annual Year Reports
Tata Consultancy Services Ltd.
Infosys Technology Ltd.
Wipro Ltd.
Sathyam Computers Services Ltd.
The New Indian Express - 12.11.2006
PMK's Ultimatum to Reliance's entry into retail trade.

Apendix
www.economywatch.com - sectors attracting FDI
www.plugged.in - VC Investement in India
www.Ministry of Overseas Indian.com

Index